Treating the Pathology
in the Clergy
Sexual Abuse
Crisis

Still
Unhealed

Nuala Kenny
SC, OC, MD, FRCP(C)

with David Deane

**TWENTY-THIRD
PUBLICATIONS**

NOVALIS

© 2019 Novalis Publishing Inc.

Published in Canada by Novalis
Publishing Office
1 Eglinton Avenue East, Suite 800
Toronto, Ontario, Canada
M4P 3A1

Head Office
4475 Frontenac Street
Montréal, Québec, Canada
H2H 2S2

www.novalis.ca

Cover design: Martin Gould
Cover image: Jessica Hyde / iStock
Layout: Audrey Wells

Library and Archives Canada Cataloguing in Publication

Title: Still unhealed : treating the pathology in the clergy sexual abuse crisis
    / Sister Nuala P. Kenny, M.D. with David Deane, Ph.D.
Names: Kenny, Nuala P., author. | Deane, David, 1973- author.
Identifiers: Canadiana 20190121122 | ISBN 9782896886746 (softcover)
Subjects: LCSH: Catholic Church—Clergy—Sexual behavior. | LCSH: Child sexual abuse
by clergy.

Classification: LCC BX1912.9 .K46 2019 | DDC 261.8/3272088282—dc23

We acknowledge the support of the Government of Canada.
Printed in Canada.

Published in the United States by
TWENTY-THIRD PUBLICATIONS
One Montauk Avenue, Suite 200
New London, CT 06320
(860) 437-3012 or (800) 321-0411
www.twentythirdpublications.com
ISBN: 978-1-62785-495-5

Cover design: Jeff McCall

The Scripture quotations contained herein are from the New Revised Standard Version
of the Bible, copyrighted 1989 by the Division of Christian Education of the National
Council of the Churches of Christ in the United States of America, and are used by
permission. All rights reserved.

5 4 3 2 1   23   22   21   20   19

Acknowledgements

Recognizing and responding to the pain and suffering of the victims and survivors of clergy sexual abuse of children and youth has been for me a powerful and life-changing experience. As a Religious Sister, a pediatrician with a ministry to care for, protect and promote the full human and spiritual development of children, working on this issue for over 30 years has brought me into the Paschal Mystery in a very real way.

At times I have been overwhelmed by the issue and just wanted to walk away. But I also have a strong sense of a calling to heal victims and survivors and my Church which is both holy and sinful. I could not have continued if it had not been for the faith and support of many.

First, I thank my good Irish parents for raising me in a faith deeper than structures. My former bishop and friend Archbishop James Hayes, a father of the Second Vatican Council, taught me to love the Church as the Body of Christ and a Priestly People. I am grateful to the Sisters of Charity of Halifax for their unfailing support of my ministry of healing as a physician.

I recognize the crucial role in my understanding of the issue played by Archbishop Alphonsus Penney of St. John's, Newfoundland, who invited me to participate in the ground-breaking Archdiocesan Commission of Enquiry into the Sexual Abuse of Minors by Members of the Clergy there. The Commission decided wisely to pursue not only academic research on the issue but the experience of those affected. I learned the crucial lesson of listening to victim-survivors. In a very special way I thank all the victim-survivors of clergy sexual abuse and their families who have helped me to understand their pain and who trusted that I would do what I could to foster healing and long-term prevention. The Commission taught me the importance of deeper study of the systemic and cultural issues fostering the crisis and inadequate leadership response.

I want to express special thanks to my own bishop, Anthony Mancini, Archbishop of Halifax-Yarmouth. He has been unfailingly supportive of me and wrote the foreword to my 2012 *Healing the Church: Diagnosing and Treating the Clergy Sexual Abuse Crisis.* I acknowledge the many non-offending bishops and priests who have trusted me to lead clergy study days and to share my insights on diagnosis and often uncomfortable and challenging recommendations for treatment.

I am grateful to the Canadian Conference of Catholic Bishops for their invitation to participate in their 1990–1992 deliberations and produce *From Pain to Hope* and again in 2014 to assist in their 2018 revision, *Protecting Minors from Sexual Abuse: A Call to the Catholic Faithful in Canada for Healing, Reconciliation and Transformation.* Archbishop Mancini courageously and faithfully chaired the 2014–2018 Ad Hoc Committee on this revision. Working with him was a graced experience of mutuality and respect, even when we disagreed.

Joseph Sinasac, Simon Appolloni and the staff of Novalis Publishing have been courageously supportive of my work. Anne Louise Mahoney provided wonderful editorial help. And Tim Krahn, a faithful research assistant, has again gone above the call of duty.

Sr. Nuala P. Kenny, M.D.

Contents

Chapter 3

Diagnostic Disagreements and Fractures in the Body of Christ

Chapter 4

Morally Mute: The Corruption of Silence and Denial

Chapter 5

Reformation and Renewal for a Sick Soul

Chapter 6

Healing Power and Relationships in the Church

Chapter 7

Infected by the Holy Spirit: An Ecclesiology for Healing and Renewal

Chapter 8

A Prescription for Conversion, Reform and Healing .. 145

Prayer for the future

Endnotes

Introduction

"Lord, save us! We are perishing!" And Jesus said to them, "Why are you afraid, you of little faith?" (Matthew 8:25-26)

Sexual abuse by Catholic clergy is the greatest scandal of the modern Church. It has caused devastating, life-long harm to victim-survivors and their families and communities. It has resulted in the loss of trust in the Church as a place of holiness, care and justice, and has eroded the credibility of its leaders as disciples of a loving and merciful Jesus. The power of the Church as a sacrament of salvation seems to have been severely wounded by an inherent sinfulness and the unprecedented experience of former Pope Benedict disagreeing with Pope Francis on causes and challenges. For some, it has precipitated a crisis of faith in God as it has wounded bodies and minds and crushed souls.

As a pediatrician, I am all too familiar with the devastating harms of the physical and sexual abuse of children and youth by family members and trusted others. As a Religious Sister, clergy sexual abuse has given me a totally new appreciation for the lamentations of the prophet Jeremiah: "See, O Lord, how distressed I am; my stomach churns, my heart is wrung within me" (Lamentations 1:20). I have groaned like Jeremiah and shed tears over what I have learned and experienced in 40 years working in this area. My stomach has turned in disgust at the abuse of power and trust, and at the magnitude of the harm to victims, their families, communities, non-offending clergy and to the entire Body of Christ. As a physician trained to respond rapidly to illness and risk of harm, the denial and delay in leadership

9

response has both baffled and angered me. My heart aches over the often vicious disagreement regarding the accurate and comprehensive diagnosis and treatment of the root causes of this crisis. I have prayed with some who have lost their faith and walk with many who have lost their trust in the institutional Church and its leaders. A whole new genre of stories on "why I am leaving the Church" has emerged on social media. I understand well the human temptation to just turn and walk away from this crisis.

A crisis is a critical – and, commonly – chaotic turning point. Recall the tragic images of a bustling, powerful New York City brought to its knees on 9/11, or the beauty and grandeur of New Orleans ravaged by the floods of Hurricane Katrina. In a medical crisis, life and death are on the line. We recognize these critical moments embedded in phrases such as "the fever has broken"; "we removed the whole tumour"; "she has awakened from the coma"; and "he is breathing on his own," or, tragically, "Sorry, we did all we could." I believe it is this kind of life- and holiness-threatening crisis that we are experiencing in the Church. This crisis requires the active participation of the laity and the clergy more than ever before. In his 2018 *Letter to the People of God*, Pope Francis acknowledges that "It is impossible to think of a conversion of our activity as a Church that does not include the active participation of all God's people."[1]

Goals for this book

This work is a reflection on how we, as disciples of Christ, might make sense of what has happened in this crisis and respond both individually and communally. This response requires an exploration of the lived experience of the Church with respect to the clergy sexual abuse of children and youth in order to assist in understanding the spiritual and ecclesial challenges. It aims to provide support for laity and clergy who desire repentance and continual conversion to disciples of a loving and merciful God. So, this work is rooted in the "mind of Christ" and belief in the power of the Holy Spirit to make all things new.

In the midst of the constant sensational media coverage, as dramatically experienced during the 2019 Summit in Rome, and the barrage of differing diagnoses, including that of former Pope Benedict, where is a person of faith to go? Who is to be trusted? As a medical educator, I know well the challenges of providing accurate information to patients who are inundated with advice from friends and family and advertising hype about miracle diets, age-defying medications and beauty-promising cosmetic surgery. In light of an explosion of scholarly writing on the issue of clergy sexual abuse from theology and medicine, psychology, sociology, law, anthropology and organizational studies and insights from the Summit, I aim to summarize authoritative faith-based work and relevant information and make it accessible for Catholics in their discernment.

Framing the crisis

Some clergy and laity continue in silence and denial, pressing for a return to orthodoxy. They seem to believe in a nostalgic restoration of the "good old days," when the Church was all-powerful and privileged. They imagine a Catholic "Make the Church great again" movement as being both possible and capable of delivering the cure needed for today's Church. They seem blind to the fact that the "good old days" – with their secrecy, unquestioned obedience and abuse of power and authority – were never good for the abused. Some clergy and laity cope by doing what they can within present structures. Some attend services but withhold financial support. Others have left the Church. However, an increasing number are responding with prophetic criticism of structures and beliefs and calls for deep repentance, conversion and reform in the Church. This work is offered in support of them and their efforts at healing and renewing the Church.

My own journey with clergy sexual abuse began in 1989, in the pain and anguish of my participation in the still unique lay-led Archdiocesan Commission of Inquiry on Clergy Sexual Abuse in St. John's, Newfoundland, Canada. This Commission was called by

Archbishop Alphonsus Penney after widespread abuse at the revered Irish Christian Brothers' Mount Cashel orphanage and subsequent revelations and criminal charges against a large number of clergy. The Commission undertook an in-depth review of what was known about the sexual abuse of minors at that time. Significantly, it also committed to go to the parishes most affected by the abuse and listen to the people. I can still see and feel the rage, grief and disillusionment of the families, friends and parish communities that we were privileged to visit and listen to. It brought me new insights into the deep-rooted spiritual harms that occur when the perpetrator is a "man of God."

My original concerns were related to the treatment of victims, the support of survivors and the protection of minors. While much has been done, these are still critical issues. However, I became aware that treating and preventing the abuse required an accurate diagnosis of why and how this behaviour had occurred. My participation in a number of international meetings on the subject and in Canadian national and diocesan projects aimed at dealing with the crisis led me to understand the crucial importance of systemic and cultural factors, including organizational structure, beliefs and practices that allowed the abuse to happen and to continue unchecked. In any other organization, such chaos and devastation would be recognized as a tipping point, resulting in either dissolution or substantive reform and renewal. In theological and spiritual terms, this is a time for repentance, purification and transformation.

In 2012, moved to make some sense of the ongoing issue, promote dialogue between and among clergy and laity to break the secrecy surrounding the issue, and contribute to healing and renewal, I wrote *Healing the Church: Diagnosing and Treating the Clergy Sex Abuse Crisis.*[2]

That work confirmed the nature and severity of the harms to individual victim-survivors, but also expanded our understanding of the harms to families, communities, non-offending clergy and the entire Body of Christ. Using medical metaphors, I identified the elements necessary for healing and curing: recognition of the need for help, an accurate diagnosis, an effective and accessible treatment, and a cooperative patient in an environment that was supportive of recovery and rehabilitation. The dangers of misdiagnosis and the provision of only symptomatic relief were clearly identified. I concluded that work with some thoughts and prayers on what I judged to be a "fragile and uncertain" prognosis for healing the Church.

I had no idea just how fragile and uncertain that prognosis was.

Seven years after writing that book and 40 years after the initial public revelations in victim statements, legal cases, Commission reports and academic inquiry, and despite the development of policies and protocols, the crisis has progressed to a kind of global septic shock in the Body of Christ. This reality confirms that there has been a serious misdiagnosis of the fundamental pathology. Today it is clear that there are three interrelated elements to the crisis. First are the public revelations of the long-standing issue of clergy sexual abuse, specifically of children and youth. Second is the negligent and pastorally insensitive response of Church leaders to victims and their families and communities. Finally, there is the ongoing critical failure of Church leadership to address the underlying spiritual and cultural ecclesial factors, including beliefs, practices and organizations operative in the crisis. The inattention to underlying systemic and cultural issues has resulted in a deeper and broader crisis than originally imagined.

Pope Francis captures the climate and context in which we must try to respond to the challenges of the abuse crisis when he declares, "I see that the thing the church needs most today is the ability to heal wounds and to warm the hearts of the faithful … I see the church as a field hospital after battle…. You have to heal his wounds. Then we can talk about everything else. Heal the wounds."[3] In a field hospital, life-and-death decisions are made in situations of great risk and in the chaos of combat. The Pope's use of medical metaphors has significance for accurate diagnosis and effective healing from the wounds of clergy sexual abuse. He draws upon a tradition that sees the Church in organic terms. Gregory the Great, for example, saw sins of the members as wounds carried by the entire Church, and pastors as physicians of souls who "must tend to their own illness even as they treat the wounds of others."[4] Medical metaphors help express the real pain and suffering of abuse and help foster an empathic understanding of the depth and complexity of the wounds these crimes have caused to victims and the Body of Christ as a whole. These metaphors intuitively capture different underlying pathology: from acute illness in healthy or debilitated individuals to endemic disease that is pervasive, a multi-generational state of ill health affecting an entire community. In this work I diagnose the sickness affecting the Church in the clergy sexual abuse crisis as endemic. Because endemic illness is pervasive and multi-generational, the affected community experiences the sickness as normal.

This work builds on and expands insights articulated in *Healing the Church* and in other interdisciplinary research efforts. I am not a theologian, and I recognized that I needed help to further explore the ecclesial and theological issues required for effective interventions. For this work I consult a friend and colleague, David Deane, associate professor of theology at the Atlantic School of Theology in Halifax, Nova Scotia, for assistance in understanding some of the theological issues underlying this crisis and theological insights for conversion and reform. Accurate diagnosis of how and why this crisis has unfolded in the Church is an exercise in theology as "a process of systematic, critical-constructive reflection on the articulations, ecclesial forms and practice of faith with a view to identify their ills and strains – whether conceptual, historical, hermeneutical or practical – and seeking to enhance their quality."[5] This book focuses on the Church's historical experience of clergy sexual abuse and blends theological reflection with other traditions of inquiry, such as medicine, psychology, sociology and organizational studies for insights into reform and renewal.

Outline of this book

Chapter 1 reviews the history of the crisis, with particular attention paid to the North American experience for signs and symptoms of deep-seated spiritual and ecclesial pathology that has manifested itself in this now global crisis. The six years since the publication of *Healing the Church* and the influence of Pope Francis's leadership and identification of the "temptations of the Church" and "diseases of leadership" are assessed. Finally, there is an analysis of the 2019 Summit in Rome, with attention to its accomplishments, key statements requiring follow-up, and systemic and cultural issues, including beliefs, practices and organization that still need attention.

Chapter 2 identifies what is now known of the harms of clergy sexual abuse of minors for individual victim-survivors, drawing on heart-wrenching personal experience in biography and blog posts as well as court records and clinical research. The understanding of the harms is broadened to include families and communities, non-offending clergy and the whole Body of Christ. The dynamics of the sexual abuse crisis provide a lens for reflection on personal, systemic and cultural issues specific to abuse in the Church, including beliefs and practices, operative in the abuse and in leadership response. Particular attention is given to the lack of a theology of children and of a moral theology insensitive to the effects of our sins on others.

Chapter 3 emphasizes the importance of a correct diagnosis for effective treatment. It reviews the scholarly analysis of the complex systemic and cultural factors involved in this ecclesial crisis. The significance of some single-issue diagnoses, with particular attention to the role of Catholic moral theology and the theology of sexuality and sexual morality, are considered. The challenge of different and increasingly polarized diagnoses of the nature of the crisis, including the comments of the Pope emeritus Benedict, is clearly identified. Reclaiming the theologies of conscience, virtue and discernment is presented as elements in empowerment for healing and reform.

The powerful roles of secrecy, denial and cover-up in all elements of the crisis are the focus of chapter 4. Insights from sociology, psychology and organizational management studies regarding factors that foster moral blindness and moral muteness in the face of wrongdoing are presented. Church-specific factors enabling silence and denial are analyzed, with particular attention to canon law, moral theology, hierarchy and lack of accountability. A new commitment to meaningful dialogue in the Church is proposed as an essential element in repentance and reform.

To understand better the ongoing resistance to meaningful reform, in chapter 5 I consult Professor Deane for insights into the nature of conversion and reform for Christians and for lessons from history of effective reform in the Catholic Church. I also seek a theological understanding of the roots of resistance to meaningful reform, with particular focus on the failure to engage the reforms of the Second Vatican Council (1962–1965).

Chapter 6 explores the abuse of power and authority in this crisis. This abuse is recognized as a profound contradiction to Jesus' understanding of and witness to power and authority. The culture of the Church, the development of the sharp clergy–laity distinction, clericalism and the role of women in the Church are assessed for their roles in the crisis.

Because this crisis is not just about individual sins and failings but is a Church crisis, in chapter 7 I again consult Professor Deane for help in understanding the role of ecclesiology, which studies the basic beliefs about and practices around the nature of the Church in the unfolding of this crisis and leadership response. This history also raises crucial questions about the theology of bishops, priesthood and laity that must be addressed going forward.

Chapter 8 reviews the elements of a prescription for conversion, reform and healing. It reaffirms that the primary diagnosis of the abuse crisis is personal and ecclesial contradiction to the words and witness of Jesus. The first element is repentance, with a firm commitment to making atonement. Reflection on personal and ecclesial conversion in this work dramatically demonstrates that moving from apologies to amends and atonement requires changes in our discourse, doctrine and structures. An effective prescription demands an accurate diagnosis; this work demonstrates the forces of divisive and polarizing diagnoses that are fracturing the Body of Christ. So, there is an urgent need for prayerful discernment by clergy and laity together as we accept the challenge of areas in need of reform to restore healthy function and to correct deformities in the Body of Christ. This restoration means involvement from the highest levels in the Church to dioceses and parishes and individual disciples, as well as profound trust in the power of the Holy Spirit to "make all things new" (Revelation 21:5). Finally, healing requires a cooperative patient in a supportive environment. Internal divisions, the loss of Church credibility and the decline of the religious in increasingly secular societies make the environment hostile rather than supportive. The always risky act of giving a prognosis calls for great courage and trust in the power of God to save and restore.

A closing word

This work uses the language of healing, not curing, intentionally. There will never be a total cure for our individual and communal moral failures. Conversion, healing and renewal can only come from responses carried out in Spirit-infused ways that are rooted in Jesus' words, witness and Paschal Mystery. Only the power of the Holy Spirit can help us rise above corrosive liberal–conservative divisions. This book seeks to contribute to the ongoing conversion, reformation and empowerment of disciples of Christ and to the practical organizational change that is needed to promote healing of these pathologies and prevention of a recurrence.

Chapter 1

Spiritual and Ecclesial Pathologies Manifested in the Clergy Sexual Abuse Crisis

"Those who are well have no need of a physician, but those who are sick [do]." (Matthew 9:12)

Introduction

Jesus' entire ministry can be understood as one of healing and reconciliation. The leper says, "'Lord, if you choose, you can make me clean.' Then Jesus stretched out his hand, touched him, and said, 'I do choose. Be made clean.' Immediately the leprosy left him" (Luke 5:12-13). Families and friends who are desperate to help a loved one cut a hole in the roof to bring the man to the great healer (Mark 2:3-4). The outcast woman with the hemorrhage only wants to touch the hem of his garment (Mark 5:25-34; Luke 8:43-48). The grief of the widow of Nain at the death of her son (Luke 7:11-17) and of Jesus' friends Martha and Mary on the death of their brother Lazarus (John 11:1-25) moves Jesus, as does the faith of Jairus when his young daughter is dying (Matthew 9:18-26; Mark 5:21-43; Luke 8:40-56). There are three elements to all of Jesus' healings: response to the physical suffering; restoration of a sense of dignity and worth to the person; and return of the sick and often isolated individual to the love and support of family and community. Today, victims of clergy sexual abuse, their families and communities, and the entire Body of Christ are crying out for this kind of healing.

Healing requires an accurate and comprehensive diagnosis. All diagnosis begins in the experience of the one who is ill or suffering. A medical case history is not history in the classic sense of a biography or epic. A medical history is focused on identifying patterns of physical signs, such as bruising and swelling, and patient symptoms, such as pain and weakness, to come to an accurate diagnosis of the pathology. Pathology is the study of the underlying causes and consequences of illness. The history begins with careful attention to the patient's story: when the symptoms began and how they have progressed; what makes them worse or relieves them; and what kind of help the patient has already sought. There is also inquiry into the family and social history, as well as environmental factors for their possible role. The challenge is to focus on what is relevant for diagnosis, but not so narrowly as to ignore other vital details.

We begin our search for healing and renewal by exploring the history of the clergy abuse crisis, with particular attention to the experience of the Church in the United States and Canada, then Ireland and Australia and globally. Perspective and personal history matter in both the writing and reading of history. I do so as an American born and raised in New York to devout Irish immigrants in the "glory days." The church was the centre of family and community life, with baptisms, marriages, first communions, confirmations and parochial school events. I was taught in high school by the Sisters of Charity of Halifax, Nova Scotia, and went to Canada for my religious formation. I entered religious life the month the Second Vatican Council began in 1962, and I saw the election of a Catholic as president of the United States. It was a heady and exciting time. But we now know there was a dark side to the history.

We explore the history of clergy sexual abuse not simply to repeat and lament the now familiar horrific details, but to identify key signs and symptoms for their insights into underlying spiritual and ecclesial pathology operative in the crisis.[1] As we know from experience in health care, the listing of signs and symptoms revealed in a medical history can be very private, intimate, even humiliating. Symptoms can be embarrassing, and the medical history can elicit complex and sensitive issues regarding our own behaviours and lifestyle that contributed to our sickness.

Our goals in this chapter are to review the history of the clergy abuse crisis for signs and symptoms of some deep-seated spiritual and ecclesial pathology manifested there. Then we assess the nature and adequacy of early Church leadership responses and identify the shift in focus to systemic and cultural issues in the Pope Francis era and the significance of his 2019 Summit. Finally, we reflect on implications of the increasingly vitriolic and polarizing divisions in the Church for conversion, reform and healing.

The history of clergy sexual abuse

The history is explored in four time periods: the early history, contemporary public revelations, the Pope Francis era, and achievements and ongoing challenges arising from the 2019 Summit in Rome.

In contrast to popular belief that the abuse crisis is a product of modern sexually permissive societies, clerical sexual abuse of minors is a long-standing problem. It is addressed in medieval penitentiaries and decrees as early as the Council of Elvira (306) and in the original *Corpus Juris Canonici*, where such abuse is a *grave derelict* or serious sin.[2] Three characteristics that will dominate the history emerge: debates regarding the "privilege of the clergy" to be tried exclusively in Church courts, unaccountable to civil law; secrecy and avoidance of scandal, as in Pope Pius XI's 1922 decree *Crimen Sollicitationis*, which placed abuse of minors under the "Secret of the Holy Office" and Pope Paul VI's 1974 *Secreta Continere*, which renamed this the "Pontifical Secret"; and the focus on the offending cleric rather than on victims. This last element was exemplified in 1051, when the great reformer St. Peter Damian appealed to Pope Leo IX to take strong action against clerical sexual contact with young boys. It is noted that "Although Peter had paid significant attention to the impact of offending clerics on their victims, the Pope focused only on the sinfulness of the clerics and their need to repent."[3] The *1983 Code of Canon Law* continued to privilege this pastoral approach to priests. Inattention to the harm done to vulnerable youth is an early and enduring feature. Crucially important for diagnosis is the fact that this crisis is not a recent event, but an issue the Church has dealt with internally and in secrecy for generations.

In the 1960s, concerns about the effective treatment of sexual offenders were raised by leaders at the Paraclete Center in New Mexico. Houses of Affirmation in the United States developed to help troubled priests, especially with alcohol addiction. In 1978, Pope John Paul II was elected; he served as Pontiff until his death in 2005, governing the response to the clergy abuse crisis for almost 30 years. The contemporary public crisis began in 1983, with public disclosures of the clergy sexual abuse of minors and the criminal conviction of clergy in the United States and Canada. There are many sources for this history. Revelations arose not from some deep examination by Church leadership of the long-standing problem or from the acknowledgement of the emerging secular evidence of the harms of the sexual abuse of minors, but through the activities of lawyers in criminal and civil cases[4] and as a result of work by investigative journalists.[5] Following the highly public case of Fr. Gilbert Gauthe in Louisiana, Arthur Jones, Jason Berry and others at the *National Catholic Reporter* (NCR) consolidated a report on other cases emerging in the US, Canada and Ireland, warning of the harmful consequences if bishops did not deal with this issue.[6]

In May 1985, before the NCR exposé, Fr. Thomas Doyle, a canonist for the papal nuncio in Washington, Fr. Michael Peterson, director of St. Luke Institute, a treatment facility for clergy, and Ray Mouton, a lawyer, presented a comprehensive analysis of the clergy sexual abuse issue to the annual gathering of the US bishops.[7] The bishops tabled the report and did not issue a public statement until their 1988 *Pedophilia Statement*. It frames abuse as a societal issue, with no mention of the emerging Church experience.

The crisis was not contained to the United States. In 1989, Archbishop Alphonsus Penney of St. John's, Newfoundland, Canada, convened a unique lay-led Commission to advise him on catastrophic abuse in that city. It concluded that "no single cause can account for the sexual abuse … rather, that a combination of factors coincided to allow the abuse to occur."[8] It identified issues in urgent need of further study, including abuse of power, education of clergy and laity, sexuality, support of priests, and the Church's approach to avoid scandal. In 1992, an Ad Hoc Committee of the Canadian Conference of Catholic Bishops (CCCB) produced *From Pain to Hope*, the first national guidelines to identify the importance of systemic and cultural issues in the crisis.[9] There was no formal follow-up of these issues.

In 1992, the United States Conference of Catholic Bishops (USCCB) approved its voluntary guidelines, *The Five Principles*, "… to respond promptly to allegations, if there is evidence to relieve offender of duties and refer for assessment and treatment, comply with civil law, reach out to victims, families and communities and deal as openly as possible with the issue."[10] However, Pope John Paul II did not issue a public statement on the escalating crisis until his June 1993 Letter to the US Bishops, which began with an expression of sympathy for the suffering the scandal had caused the bishops. Victims were given passing reference. The Pope spoke of the abuse in the context of sin, culture and media bias against the Church, with no acknowledgement of any deeper ecclesial issue or a global crisis.

In June 2002, the USCCB produced its Charter for the Protection of Children and Young People.[11] In October of that year, Rome rejected some elements of the Charter, wanting a strict definition of sex abuse, preservation of the statutes of limitation on civil liability and limited authority of lay oversight. That same year, 20 years after the public revelations, the clergy abuse issue erupted in Boston, Massachusetts, with the investigation of more than 90 priests of the archdiocese.[12] The Academy Award–winning film *Spotlight* dramatically portrays the horrified reporters' reactions as they came to grips with the magnitude of the abuse and leadership response. Following an outcry regarding his mismanagement and cover-up of cases, Cardinal Archbishop Law's resignation was finally accepted by Pope John Paul II in December 2002. Cardinal Law was not penalized for mismanagement; he was appointed Arch-Priest of Saint Mary Major, one of the four major basilicas in Rome. This was seen by many as an affirmation in the face of episcopal failure.

In 2004, the National Review Board set up by the United States Conference of Catholic Bishops to monitor the abuse situation identified characteristics of US Church officials' response as a failure to recognize the magnitude of the harm to victims, presumptions in favour of accused priests, secrecy and avoidance of scandal, dependence on the therapeutic model, reliance on attorneys, clericalism, and lack of episcopal accountability. It concluded that "This is a failing not simply on the part of the priests who sexually abused minors but also on the part of those bishops and other church leaders who did not act effectively to preclude abuse in the first instance or respond appropriately when it occurred."[13] The first of two reports commissioned by the John Jay College of Criminal Justice identifying the nature and scope of the crisis was released.[14]

Despite this devastating history, the June 2009 – June 2010 Year of the Priest began with a triumphal celebration of St. John Vianney's teaching that "the priest is everything" and ended somberly with Pope Benedict's May 2010 revision of the motu proprio *Sacramentorum Sanctitatis tutela* to include clergy sexual abuse of minors. There was no recognition of any links between the exaltation of priests and the abuse crisis.

At the October 2012 Synod of Bishops, Bishop Brian Dunn of Antigonish, Nova Scotia, Canada, a diocese with tragic experience of clergy sexual abuse, called the bishops "... to consider why this crisis has happened. It is important that we make the proper diagnosis of the issues involved, so that we can decide on the most appropriate strategies." There was no mention of Bishop Dunn's intervention or of the abuse crisis itself in official Synod reports.

Pope Benedict XVI seemed to have come to an understanding of the depth and complexity of the crisis from reviewing reports of clergy abuse worldwide that were submitted to the Congregation of the Doctrine of the Faith.[15] His 2010 Letter to the Catholic faithful of Ireland states:

> Only by examining carefully the many elements that gave rise to the present crisis can a clear-sighted diagnosis of its causes be undertaken and effective remedies be found. Certainly, among the contributing factors we can include: inadequate procedures for determining the suitability of candidates for the priesthood and the religious life; insufficient human, moral, intellectual and spiritual formation in seminaries and novitiates; a tendency in society to favour the clergy and other authority figures; and a misplaced concern for the reputation of the Church and the avoidance of scandal, resulting in failure to apply existing canonical penalties and to safeguard the dignity of every person. Urgent action is needed to address these factors ....[16]

In his 2010 Christmas greeting to the Curia, after more revelations of clergy sexual abuse, he declared that

> We must accept this humiliation as an exhortation to truth and a call to renewal. Only the truth saves. We must ask ourselves what we can do to repair as much as possible the injustice that has occurred. We must ask ourselves what was wrong in our proclamation, in our whole way of living the Christian life, to allow such a thing to happen.[17]

In 2006, after many egregious charges of all types of sexual abuse since 1988, he forced Fr. Marcial Marciel Degollado, the Pope John Paul II–supported founder of the Legionaries of Christ, into seclusion, and punished many offenders.

In Ireland, the 2009 Report into the Catholic Archdiocese of Dublin (the Murphy Report) represented the culmination of four public inquiries following widespread abuse that emerged in Ireland in the 1970s. It also identified characteristics of leadership response as "… the maintenance of secrecy, the avoidance of scandal, the protection of the reputation of the Church, and the preservation of its assets. All other considerations, including the welfare of children and justice for victims, were subordinated to these priorities."[18] The report detailed structures and rules of the Church that facilitated cover-up. Pope Benedict's 2010 Letter to the Irish faithful admitted that "grave errors of judgment were made and failures of leadership occurred," but failed to address the role of these structures and rules in the devastating experience of the Irish Church.

The Australian Royal Commission into Institutional Responses to Child Sexual Abuse was conducted over five years. It found that in Catholic Church institutions, more children were abused than in any other church, charitable or privately owned institution. It concluded there were "catastrophic failures of leadership of Catholic Church authorities over many decades, particularly before 1990s."[19] The Commission examined systemic and cultural issues including clericalism, poor education programs in seminaries, and abuse of power. On December 12, 2018, Cardinal George Pell, a member of Pope Francis's Council and prefect of the Secretariat for the Economy, was found guilty on five charges of "historical child sexual offenses" and sentenced to prison. As this book was going to press, he was awaiting a ruling on his appeal of the conviction. Church leadership has struggled to implement most of the Commission recommendations. Institutional defensiveness and inertia remain significant challenges despite intense public scrutiny and loss of credibility for the Church.

The June 24, 2019, "ad limina" visit of the Australian bishops to Rome directly addresses the humiliation of the crisis and the need for humility and hope.

Pope Benedict XVI renounced the papacy on February 28, 2013, for reasons of health. He became Archbishop Emeritus of Rome and promised to retreat from public life and serve the Church through a life dedicated to prayer.

The nature and adequacy of Church leadership responses

Over the time of public revelations of the crisis, Church leadership slowly but gradually responded with revisions of canon law, policies and protocols for responding to allegations against priests, promotion of safe ministry programs and forensic audits, and background checks of Church workers. These are necessary approaches today. However, they continue the bureaucratic approach despite evidence of the persistent failure of Church leadership to comply with long-standing canons and established protocols, as well as evidence of outright cover-up and disregard for the rules.[20] Psychological screening for the seminary was improved and a curriculum on human formation added to priestly formation.[21]

These important responses focus on the sin, sickness and crimes of individual priest offenders. However, they fail to reflect critically on the underlying systemic and cultural issues and Church leadership responses and accountability. Fr. Thomas Doyle, who has studied this issue since its public revelation in the 1980s, has observed that "In spite of the number of recorded clergy abuse cases throughout the world, the official Church refuses or is unable to make any connection between the clerical abuse crisis and the internal structural dynamics of the Catholic Church."[22]

The Pope Francis era

From his emergence on the balcony at St. Peter's, Pope Francis brought a humble, pastoral approach to the papacy. As a Jesuit, he also brought a unique capacity for discernment of systemic and cultural factors operative in the crisis. At the July 2013 Latin American Episcopal Conference (CELAM) in Rio de Janeiro, he identified some "temptations" of the Church: understanding the gospel as an ideology rather than a call to discipleship; functionalism, which reduces the Church to a non-governmental organization concerned with efficiency and leaving no room for transcendence; and clericalism, a particular temptation of clergy regarding privilege and power that includes complicit laity. When falling prey to these temptations, he recognized that the Church can adopt practices and habits, and even enshrine them in structures, that impede its capacity to serve its essential mission. In an address to the German bishops, he later warned that a Church that is understood in terms of a structure scarred by organizational problems that can be healed by structural or procedural solutions is a heresy "… which puts its trust in administrative structures, in perfect organizations."

In an extraordinary Christmas message at the end of his second year as Pope in 2014, Francis did not engage in the usual pleasantries but said, "The Curia … like every human body is exposed to disease, malfunction and infirmity." He called for a "real examination of conscience" and warned bluntly of 15 separate "diseases" in their work and attitudes, including feelings of being immortal, immune or indispensable; a pathology of power and narcissism; a spiritual Alzheimer's in losing the memory of our personal salvation history and a decline of spiritual faculties; an existential schizophrenia of hypocrisy; mental and spiritual petrification in hearts of stone; and the cancer of closed circles and careerism."

In 2013, Pope Francis announced the creation of the Pontifical Commission on Protection of Minors; it was met with such resistance by senior officials at the Vatican that he issued a letter calling for their close and complete cooperation with the Commission. Marie Collins, a clergy abuse survivor and champion for the voices of victims, later resigned from the Commission, citing her "frustration at a lack of cooperation with the commission by other offices in the Roman Curia."[23] Despite disappointment regarding its early achievements, the Commission was very influential in organizing the 2019 Summit.

After a short-lived retreat from public life, in November 2016, in a book-length interview with journalist Peter Seewald, former Pope Benedict defended his 2005–2013 papacy from criticism.

In December 2016, on the feast of the Holy Innocents, Pope Francis wrote to bishops acknowledging the pain of victims and the sins of denial and cover-up. He called for them "… to find the courage needed to take all necessary measures and to protect in every way the lives of our children, so that such crimes may never be repeated. In this area, let us adhere, clearly and faithfully, to 'zero tolerance.'" Despite Pope Francis's commitment, the issue continued to fester.

In 2018, the fifth anniversary of Francis's pontificate, the public crisis continued to escalate, with a new focus on episcopal leaders who had been found guilty or were under investigation for sexual abuse and cover-up. These included Cardinals George Pell (Australia), Francisco Javier Errázuriz (Chile) and Laurent Monsengwo Pasinya (Democratic Republic of the Congo); Bishop Robert Finn of Kansas City–St. Joseph, Missouri; Archbishop Philip Wilson of Adelaide, Australia; and the criminal trial of Cardinal Philippe Barbarin of Lyon, France, who was exonerated but has since submitted his resignation to Pope Francis. Three events escalate the pain and suffering of the Body of Christ to a full-blown state of septic shock. In his January 2018 visit to Chile, Pope Francis met with victims and apologized for "irreparable damage" that abusive priests had inflicted on them, but then defended Bishop Juan Barros Madrid of Osorno, Chile, who was accused of protecting Fr. Fernando Karadima, who was defrocked for horrendous abuse during the 1980s and 1990s. Succumbing to the pattern of protection of a cleric, the Pope said he had no proof of Bishop Barros's abuse of office and that the accusers were guilty of calumny. Cardinal Sean O'Malley of Boston, in an unprecedented display of fraternal correction, stated that the Pontiff's defense of Barros was a source of great pain for survivors and that doubt about the truth of their testimony "abandon[s] those who have suffered reprehensible criminal violations of their human dignity."[24]

The Pope accepted the fraternal correction and sent Archbishop Charles Scicluna of Malta, who was Adjunct Secretary of the Congregation for the Doctrine of the Faith, to Chile to listen to victims. After reviewing his 2,300-page report, Pope Francis admitted his error, invited survivors to Rome and met with them. He then called the bishops of Chile to Rome to discuss the Scicluna report. Subsequently, the entire Chilean episcopacy offered its resignation; Francis has accepted eight so far. On May 31, 2018, he sent an apology to "the Pilgrim people of God in Chile"[25] and acknowledged "serious mistakes in the assessment and perception of the situation, especially due to a lack of truthful and balanced information."[26]

An August 2018 Pennsylvania Grand Jury Report provided in excruciating detail the mismanagement of the sexual abuse of more than 1,000 minors by more than 300 priests covering eight dioceses.[27] Distrusting internal investigation, many US states plan to instigate similar civil inquiries. Almost all media stories were based on the 12-page introduction and sickening stories of abuse, most of which occurred decades ago, before the 2002 Dallas Charter.

Retired Washington, DC, Cardinal Theodore McCarrick then submitted an unprecedented resignation from the cardinalate and public ministry after a Congregation of the Doctrine of the Faith penal process found him guilty of sins against the sixth commandment against children and adults, most notably in well-known scandalous abuse of seminarians. This resulted in his dismissal from the clerical state. This situation fostered the scapegoating of homosexuals as the cause of the crisis. His rise to the highest ranks in the Church despite horrific abuse of seminarians demonstrated that clergy sexual abuse extends far beyond minors and includes vulnerable adults such as seminarians and women.

In 2018, the Canadian Conference of Catholic Bishops produced a revision of their 1992 guidelines, entitled *Protecting Minors from Sexual Abuse: A Call to the Catholic Faithful in Canada for Healing, Reconciliation and Transformation.*[28] It acknowledges mistakes made and lessons learned, and commits to zero tolerance of the abuse of minors. Importantly, it recognizes that "Within the Church, the goal of prevention is first and foremost a call to conversion. Firstly, this entails identifying longstanding institutional practices linked to sexual abuse; and secondly, it involves transforming those practices, ensuring that they are more closely aligned with the gospel and the Church's mission." These new guidelines made the prognosis that "The need for healing and reconciliation, for repentance and conversion, and for deep ecclesial renewal remain a challenge." Finally, they identified the principles of responsibility, accountability and transparency as essential in moving forward.

Amid increasing criticism that Pope Francis was more talk than action, the Pope wrote an extraordinary *Letter to the People of God* in August 2018 to

> acknowledge once more the suffering endured by many minors due to sexual abuse, the abuse of power and the abuse of conscience perpetrated by a significant number of clerics and consecrated persons. Crimes that inflict deep wounds of pain and powerlessness, primarily among the victims, but also in their family members and in the larger community of believers and nonbelievers alike. Looking back to the past, no effort to beg pardon and to seek to repair the harm done will ever be sufficient. Looking ahead to the future, no effort must be spared to create a culture able to prevent such situations from happening, but also to prevent the possibility of their being covered up and perpetuated. ... Every one of the baptized

should feel involved in the ecclesial and social change that we so greatly need. This change calls for a personal and communal conversion that makes us see things as the Lord does.[29]

An October 2018 Synod of Bishops on Young People, the Faith and Vocational Discernment concluded with a call for the inclusion of women in its all-male decision-making structures – "a duty of justice" that requires a "courageous change of culture."[30]

Pope Francis unexpectedly convened an unprecedented Summit in Rome for February 21-24, 2019. It aimed at addressing the crisis openly and definitively and beginning to restore the credibility of the Church as an agent of God's love, mercy, justice and protection of the most vulnerable among us. The Pope gathered the presidents of the world's 114 conferences of Catholic bishops and Eastern rite synods in Rome, together with victims of clergy abuse, Religious women and men, and lay experts in a gathering with a "synodal dimension." Synodality requires the participation of all the baptized at every level – in parishes, dioceses, and national and regional ecclesial bodies – in a discernment and reform that permeates the Church.

He created a high-level planning committee of experienced members, including Archbishop Scicluna, Cardinal Oswald Gracias (Bombay), Cardinal Blase Cupich (Chicago) and Fr. Hans Zollner, president of the Centre for Child Protection at the Pontifical Gregorian University and member of the Pontifical Commission for the Protection of Minors. The themes for the Summit were those identified by the Canadian Conference of Catholic Bishops' 2018 document: responsibility, accountability and transparency. There were enormous expectations for the Summit and so, not surprisingly, mixed evaluations of its success. Some key accomplishments, significant comments made by presenters requiring follow-up, and underlying systemic and cultural issues – including beliefs, practices and organization – that fostered the crisis are identified here.

The meeting is in itself a remarkable achievement, made possible by Pope Francis's care and concern. The candid admission of leadership failure, the commitment to move from talk to action, and the recognition of a need for the deep personal and communal conversion of all were made clear in his August 2018 Letter to the People of God:

> I am conscious of the effort and work being carried out in various parts of the world to come up with the necessary means to ensure the safety and protection of the integrity of children and of vulnerable adults, as well as implementing zero tolerance and ways of making all those who perpetrate or cover up these crimes accountable. We have delayed in applying these actions and sanctions that are so necessary ....[31]

In his opening remarks at the Summit, he added that "The holy People of God looks to us, and expects from us not simple and predictable condemnations, but concrete and effective measures to be undertaken. We need to be concrete."[32]

The Holy Father identified victims as central to the process. The first item after the Pope's opening was the viewing of a video with the testimonies of five victims. Victims also spoke during the prayer services at the end of each day. Participants heard heart-wrenching stories of abuse, including from a male victim in Chile who was rejected and treated as a liar when he revealed his abuse; a woman who had been abused for 15 years, from the age of 13, who was beaten and forced to have an abortion three times; and a nun from Asia who spoke of religious superiors who covered up abuse of nuns to avoid the wrath of bishops. Cardinal Luis Tagle of Manila then gave an emotional reflection on the pain of victims and the failure of responsibility of bishops, "… leaving a deep wound in our relationship with those we are sent to serve."

Cardinal Cupich recognized that

> None of the structural elements we enact as a synodal Church, important as they are, can guide us forward faithfully in Christ unless we anchor all our deliberations in the piercing pain of those who have been abused and of the families who

have suffered with them. The Church ... must truly be *Pietà*, broken in suffering, consoling in enveloping love, constant in pointing to the divine tenderness of God amidst the pangs of desolation in those who have been crushed by clergy abuse.

Archbishop Scicluna, an investigator and prosecutor of abuse cases in the Church, spoke to known best practices for responding to allegations of abuse and for preventing it. He said, "The faith community under our care should know that we mean business ... We will engage them with candor and humility. We will protect them at all cost. We will lay down our lives for the flock entrusted to us." This commitment is in stark contrast to the self-protection that has characterized the history of sexual abuse in the Church.

Cardinal Gracias laid out the devastating consequences of sexual abuse of minors perpetrated by clerics and others serving in the Church, which

> results in incalculable damage that is both direct and indirect ... This direct damage can be physical. Inevitably, it is psychological with all the long-term consequences of any serious emotional trauma related to a profound betrayal of trust. Very often, it is a form of direct spiritual damage that shakes faith and severely disrupts the spiritual journey of those who suffer abuse, sometimes spiralling them into despair. The indirect damage of abuse often results from failure to listen to victims or to take their claims seriously, not extending care and support to victims and their families, giving priority to protecting institutional and financial concerns (for example, by "hiding" abuse and abusers) over and above the care of victims ... the indirect damage inflicted by those with directive responsibility within the Church can be worse by re-victimising those who have already suffered abuse.

Colombian Cardinal Rubén Salazar Gómez directly rejected the excuse that this is just a societal issue, saying, "The fact that abuses occur in other institutions and groups can never justify the occurrence of abuses in the Church. There is no possible justification for not denouncing, not unmasking, not courageously and forcefully confronting any abuse that presents itself within our Church."

Cardinal Cupich further stated,

> Only a synodal vision, rooted in discernment, conversion and reform at every level can bring to the Church the comprehensive action in the defense of the most vulnerable in our midst to which God's grace is calling us ... and demands that bishops and religious superiors reject a clerical worldview that sees charges of clergy sexual abuse cast against a backdrop of status and immunities for those in the clerical state. Authentic Christ-like accompaniment sees all as equal in the Lord, and structures rooted in accompaniment make all feel and appear equal in the Lord.

Dr. Linda Ghisoni, Undersecretary for the Laity at the Dicastery for the Laity, Family and Life, situated accountability and transparency

> in the nature of the Church as a mystery of communion founded in the Trinity. As People of God on their journey, that does not avoid, but faces, with renewed communitarian awareness, even the challenges related to the abuses occurring inside to the detriment of the young undermining and breaking this communion ... demands and urges that all the members of this People, each in their own way, live consequently, the rights and duties to which they have been made to partake in baptism.

In an emotional high point of the event, Nigerian Sr. Veronica Openibo, Leader of the Society of the Holy Child Jesus and member of the executive of the International Union of Superiors General, spoke directly to Pope Francis:

At the present time, we are in a state of crisis and shame. We have seriously clouded the grace of the Christ-mission. Is it possible for us to move from fear of scandal to truth? ... With a heavy and sad heart, I think of all the atrocities we have committed as members of the Church ...We must acknowledge that our mediocrity, hypocrisy and complacency have brought us to this disgraceful and scandalous place we find ourselves as a Church. We pause to pray *Lord have mercy on us!*

Valentina Alazraki, a journalist for Mexico's Televisa news who has covered the Vatican for many years, said, "We journalists know that abuse is not limited to the Catholic Church, but you must understand that we have to be more rigorous with you than with others, by virtue of your moral role." She went on to identify "perhaps the most terrible case that happened in the Church, that of Marcial Maciel, the Mexican founder of the Legion of Christ ... as [an] emblematic case of unhealthy, corrupt communication." She concluded,

Secrecy, in the sense of an excessive tendency toward secrecy, is strictly tied to the abuse of power: it is like a safety net for those who abuse power. Today our societies have adopted transparency as a general rule, and the public believes that the only reason not to be transparent is the desire to conceal something negative or corrupt.

Germany's Cardinal Rheinhard Marx acknowledged cover-up, saying,

Files that could have documented the terrible deeds and named those responsible were destroyed, or not even created. Instead of the perpetrators, the victims were regulated and silence imposed on them. The stipulated procedures and processes for the prosecution of offences were deliberately not complied with, but instead cancelled or overridden. The rights of victims were effectively trampled underfoot. ... There are no

35

alternatives to traceability and transparency. However, there are objections which should be considered. They are mainly directed against violations of pontifical secrecy, as well as ruining the reputation of innocent priests or of the priesthood and the Church as a whole through false accusations, if these are spread.

In contrast to the long history of ignoring or rejecting findings on abuse from a range of secular studies, in his concluding remarks Pope Francis reviewed best practices formulated under the guidance of the World Health Organization and the Pontifical Commission for the Protection of Minors. He noted, "The best results and the most effective resolution that we can offer to the victims, to the People of Holy Mother Church and to the entire world, are the commitment to personal and collective conversion, the humility of learning, listening, assisting and protecting the most vulnerable...."

In celebrating the closing Mass, Archbishop Mark Coleridge of Brisbane, Australia, said,

> In these days we have been on Calvary ... In the end, there remains only the voice of the Risen Lord, urging us not to stand gazing at the empty tomb, wondering in our perplexity what to do next. Nor can we stay in the upper room where he says, *"Peace be with you"* (John 20:19). He breathes on us and the fire of a new Pentecost touches us (Acts 2:2) ... A mission stretches before us – a mission demanding not just words but real concrete action.

In April 2019, following this Summit that identified a number of critical doctrinal and organizational issues operative in the clergy sexual abuse crisis, former Pope Benedict produced an unfortunate essay on his diagnosis of the crisis.[33] This rambling document contains inexplicable comments about violence and "sex films" and social approval of pedophilia. It is totally at odds with his 2010 Letter to the People of Ireland and his 2010 Christmas Greetings to the Curia, where he identifies deep and broad systemic issues. It is also in contradiction to the long history of this problem. He blames the crisis on the sexual revolution of the 1960s and theological developments after the Second Vatican Council, specifically in the area of moral theology. He also failed to follow the Congregation for Bishops' advice to retired bishops: "The Bishop Emeritus will be careful not to interfere in any way, directly or indirectly, in the governance of the diocese. He will want to avoid every attitude and relationship that could even hint at some kind of parallel authority to that of the diocesan Bishop, with damaging consequences for the pastoral life and unity of the diocesan community."[34] Confused and hurting members of the Church have been further damaged, polarized by his actions and paralyzed in responding.

The Vatican Summit's work to ensure that laws and concrete actions are put in place is just beginning. On March 29, 2019, Pope Francis approved a new set of laws and guidelines concerning child protection for Vatican City State and for the Church's global ambassadors. Six weeks later, on May 9, he issued sweeping new norms for the investigation of clergy and religious sexual abuse in a brief Apostolic Letter, "Vos Estis Lux Mundi" (You are the light of the world).[35] It mandates every diocese in the world to develop concrete procedures for reporting the sexual abuse of minors, child pornography, and abuse of others – such as seminarians, religious women and lay women – with the motu proprio entering into force on June 1, 2019. It creates a new process for metropolitan archbishops to have authority to investigate bishops who are guilty of abuse or cover-up of abuse. This is a major step forward, but it fails to require lay participation in investigations and oversight. The Church has not lacked canons and procedures and policies on this issue. It has failed in implementation. That move requires conversion and a major cultural change at the heart of the Church.

Pope Francis's advisory council of cardinals was given the task of rewriting the Vatican's apostolic constitution and refounding the

Roman curia as an essential element in such cultural change. The final report, *Praedicate Evangelium,* consolidates dicasteries in Rome and puts them at the service of both the Pope and bishops. This represents a major cultural shift in mindset from understanding the Curia as the legal enforcement arm of the papacy and moves to its role in evangelization around three principles: colllegiality, synodality, and subsidiarity.

Meanwhile, in May 2019, Pope Francis commented on the lack of consensus in the report on the role of women deacons in the Church and stated that without it, he cannot move forward on an issue of sacramental ordination.[36]

Pathology manifested in the history needing discernment toward conversion, reformation and healing

Cultural transformation is urgently needed: the clergy sexual abuse crisis has manifested pathology in the Church and its leadership. This pathology has resulted in the unfolding of the abuse of minors and inadequate leadership response. The pathology has revealed itself in other areas of Church life and decisions in ways that are contradictory to the mind of Christ (see Philippians 2:5). Questions arising directly from the crisis demand deep theological reflections on the nature of the Church and of discipleship. These include the following:

> ‣ In a Church that is committed to the protection of life, why the egregious failure of protection of vulnerable children and youth? Why the failure of recognition of the magnitude of the life-long harm done to the health, well-being and faith of victims of clergy sexual abuse?

> ‣ What was the role of a sin-centred, act-oriented moral theology focused on the sinner who could be forgiven? How can we move from morality focused on obeying laws and rules and focus on virtue and the conscience formation necessary for discernment?

> How has our anthropology, sexual theology and sexual morality played a role?

> Why have secrecy and denial been so powerful? How can we promote dialogue and meaningful participation in the formation of doctrine and decisions at every level by clergy and laity, men and women?

> Why has our use of power and authority been so contradictory to that of Jesus? What factors need to be addressed to eliminate clericalism in the Church?

> What ecclesiology will advance the mission of the Church? What theology of priesthood rejects clerical narcissism? What seminary formation is needed for priests of today and tomorrow?

> Why has leadership adopted a management strategy of avoidance of scandal understood as reputational loss, rather than in the scriptural sense of putting an obstacle in the way to God?

> How can we heal the polarizing divisions in the Church, which are fracturing the one Body of Christ?

> What practices of personal and communal prayer and atonement are needed for conversion of all to the mind of Christ?

In the chapters to come, each of these questions will be pondered prayerfully and with help from theology and a range of secular disciplines.

Pastoral pause and prayer

> What feelings and emotions arise in you when you hear this history?

> How significant do you think the clergy sexual abuse crisis is in the life of the Church?

> Do you think this history of the clergy abuse crisis has broader implications for the Church?

> What are your deepest prayers for yourself? For your parish and diocesan community? For the entire wounded Body of Christ?

Chapter 2

Deaf to Their Cries: The Harms of Clergy Sexual Abuse

"If any of you put a stumbling block before one of these little ones who believe in me, it would be better for you if a great millstone were fastened around your neck and you were drowned in the depth of the sea." (Matthew 18:6)

Introduction

Jesus had a special love for children. Parents often brought children to meet this wonderful healer and teacher. When the apostles sought to shoo them out of the way so that the "important" folk could meet him, Jesus wanted them near: "Let the little children come to me; do not stop them; for it is to such as these that the kingdom of God belongs" (Mark 10:14). He saw in them not only their wonder and joy, but also their utter dependence, vulnerability and trust in the goodness of others. Jesus, as the revelation of the Father's love for us, shows us how that loving Father desires the vulnerable, especially children and youth, to be cared for. He calls us to be like children – not in their physical and psychological immaturity, but in their openness to the mystery of grace. And so we see touching scenes in scripture of the gentle Jesus with children. We also see and hear his righteous anger

40

at those who would harm them in any way, especially if the harm puts "a stumbling block" before one of these little ones preventing them from coming to him.

When he comes to the end of his life, Jesus, like abused children, had the experience of someone he trusted betraying him with a kiss. "So when [the traitor] came, he went up to [Jesus] at once and said 'Rabbi!' and kissed him. Then they laid hands on him and arrested him" (Mark 14:45-47). What should be a physical sign of love turns into a weapon of destruction when Judas kisses Jesus. In an experience shared with victims of abuse, an expression of love and support becomes an act of harm and devastating betrayal for Jesus.

The sexual abuse of children and youth is an egregious abuse of power, trust and authority. As we have seen in the history outlined in chapter 1, insensitivity to the magnitude of the harms done by persons who represent Jesus, and the failure to protect the most vulnerable among us, is at the heart of the ecclesial pathology manifest in this crisis and a profound contradiction to the model of Jesus and children. History contains many heart-wrenching examples of physical, psychological and sexual abuse throughout history. Even today, many children and youth around the world are forced to work in horrific conditions, serve as child soldiers in violent conflict or are trafficked for child prostitution and pornography. While most children in North American and other technologically advanced nations of the world enjoy extraordinary advantages, socio-economic status does not protect them from abuse. The Church's credibility as a force combatting this violence has been destroyed.

As a pediatrician, I have had direct experience with the physical and sexual abuse of children and youth by family members and other persons in positions of trust. I have held a trembling 12-year-old who would not lie on the emergency room examining table so the surgeon could assess the damage to his bleeding rectum from rape. I have also tried to comfort distraught parents of an abused child who were wracked with guilt and kept crying out, "How could this have happened? Why to my child?" In clinical practice I was involved with child and youth victims who came from families with status and security and victims who came from appalling life experiences of neglect and abandonment. I never cared directly for a victim of clergy sexual abuse, but have met many survivors and listened to their stories.

In this chapter, we review a brief summary of what is now known about the psychological, emotional and spiritual harms of clergy sexual abuse of children and youth. These harms are first and foremost to victim-survivors and include the immediate harms of the assault, the long-term consequences, the additional spiritual harms when the perpetrator is a "man of God," and the complexity of care and healing for survivors.

We expand the understanding of harms to include those experienced by parish and diocesan communities, non-offending clergy and the entire Body of Christ. We then explore insights on the general dynamics of how and why the sexual abuse of minors occurs, looking to research in psychology, sociology and medicine. We explore these general dynamics of clergy sexual abuse as an exercise of "faith seeking understanding" (to use St. Irenaeus's expression) for Church-specific elements operative in the abuse that require prayerful analysis leading to meaningful reform, prevention and healing. The specific focus is on the role of moral theology and the lack of a theology of children that is compatible with Jesus' words and witness.

The harms of sexual abuse of children and youth

Note: In this area, sensitivity to the language used matters. For many, the use of "victim" confirms that they were not the cause of their abuse but have been harmed. For others, "survivor" indicates that while they have been harmed, they have not been destroyed. We will use "victim" at the time of the assaults and "survivor" for those pursuing justice, compassion and healing years after the assault.

Until the late 1960s, society did not recognize the long-standing and widespread physical and sexual abuse of children and youth as serious health and social harms.[1] Ironically, the United States enacted prevention of cruelty to animal laws before child abuse laws. During my pediatric residency there was attention to a new phenomenon called Trauma X. Radiologists recognized – from x-ray patterns of old and new fractures and bruising patterns – physical abuse in young people labelled accident prone. The sexual abuse of children and youth perpetrated by family members and trusted figures took longer to recognize in large part because of the secrecy surrounding it, but also because many of the physical findings were not evident.

The physical and sexual abuse of minors, characterized by sexual activity which the minor does not comprehend, cannot consent to and is developmentally unprepared for, are now recognized as crimes as well as critical social issues in societies of the global North. Because of public education, increased social vigilance and legal constraints, there has been a decrease in North America in this kind of intimate sexual abuse, which includes a range of sexual activity: from inappropriate touching of victim and perpetrator to rape. At the same time, child pornography and trafficking and slavery are widespread. Public education about and social recognition of this issue is not yet the practice in many countries,[2] a fact that is crucially important because the Church is a global reality. The full magnitude of abuse in the Church, especially in countries and cultures that still privilege patriarchy, hierarchy and unquestioning obedience to Church authority, is unknown.

Up to 25 percent of victims demonstrate no psychological problems in childhood. However, there is now much information from clinical experience and scholarly research on the vast majority of victims who do demonstrate psychological problems.[3] This empirical research is needed to help those who deny the abuse or minimize its serious consequences. However, there are many different ways to know reality. In medicine, we have only recently given attention to narrative knowledge and the difference between the medical case history and the patient's story of illness and trauma. We have learned that the rigid genre of the medical history taught to clinicians for purposes of diagnosis focuses on the facts of physical signs and symptoms very narrowly. It intentionally filters out the messy human contexts of cause and effect. This means it fails to address many emotional, environmental and spiritual issues that are crucial to diagnosis and effective treatment.

Compassion for victims requires that we "suffer with" them (that is what the original Latin word means). We need to enter into their pain and in empathic experience try to see things from the perspective of the victim-survivor. Even more powerful than court transcripts and academic research, we now have a tragic genre of victim experiences that provides a continual reminder of the ongoing personal pain and suffering of survivors.[4] In addition to classic biographies, memoirs and autobiographies, we now have a barrage of blogs and social media stories of victims.

I include here "John's story" from *Healing the Church*. It still captures elements of the victimization that we need to understand and address today.

John's story

In 1970, John is a normal 12-year-old boy from a devout Catholic family. Fr. X, newly assigned to John's parish, is enthusiastic and charismatic. He rapidly focuses his ministry on children and youth, with particular attention to boys between 10 and 14 years of age. The priest is soon involved with many activities, from sports to altar boys and summer camps. The priest develops a particularly close relationship with John, who comes from a stable home with high Church involvement. Fr. X is a welcome guest in John's home. The family thinks nothing of sending John up to the rectory at all times to help out Fr. X. The family is happy and honoured that their boy is special to Father. John has been taught to honour the priest as the representative of Christ himself. John's trust and that of his entire family in this man of God was high.

One morning sex is introduced. After John serves Mass, Fr. X helps John remove his alb and suddenly presses himself against the boy and starts to rub himself against him. John is stunned into silence. A pattern develops. The acts escalate from fondling to oral sex and rape. Fr. X explains that what he is doing is a holy thing because he is a holy man, and John is sworn to keep this special secret between them. The abuse occurs in the rectory, in the sacristy and at the diocesan summer camp. John is shocked, confused and physically hurt. He feels that the abuse is his fault because he has in some way tempted this holy man! The same man who presides at Sunday Mass and is honoured by his family and community does these terrible things to him.

As John becomes more uncomfortable with what is happening, Fr. X threatens him and his family with eternal damnation if John tells. Finally, John reveals to his parents what is happening, and they are shocked. At first they do not believe him and John is further victimized. Then they come to understand this is all true. They go to their pastor, who says he is certain John has misunderstood Fr. X, but assures them he will take care of this. They are cautioned not to speak about the issue for fear of bringing scandal to the Church. John's parents trust that it would be taken care of.

Fr. X is called in and reprimanded; he promises not to do it again, and he is then moved to a new parish, which is given no information about his recent behaviour. John's parents are relieved to see him go. John's experience is repeated again and again with other boys in the new parish.

Neither John nor his family was given support or counselling.

No matter how many times I read this story or the many like it, I am horrified. Empathic response to John and outrage at the response overwhelm me. Anger at the parents who should have done more is also very real. The pastor's arrogance and insensitivity to the boy make me angry. I recognize that if this story happened in the 1970s and early 1980s, the pastor, like most of society, failed to understand the magnitude of the harm. It was not yet a crime, but the pastor knew that it was a sin. Secrecy is the most powerful factor in all sexual abuse, and here it is linked with the pastor's concern about avoiding scandal.

John's parents believed him in the end, and tried to act to protect him. Some parents did not believe their child when he or she reported being sexually abused by a priest; some even punished the child for slandering the priest. Some blamed the victim for the abuse and for not reporting it. Other parents might have been less vigilant about the safety of their children due to a variety of circumstances. Sometimes when parents reported abuse and the offending priest was moved to another parish, the parents remained silent, thus unwittingly participating in the risk to other children.

Research demonstrates dramatic and damaging consequences from sexual abuse during this important time in human development, including problems with the victim's sense of self, expectations and cognitive functioning. Victims' sense of self-violation is so great that they disassociate and can feel sexual stimulation and betrayal by their own bodies. They may engage in self-destructive behaviours and even suicide. The response can be erratic, from dependent to raging and angry. Cognitive function and change in school performance can continue into adulthood, with stress that causes an inability to assess the situation. Counselling near the time of the abuse can help significantly.

> John is now a barely surviving 52-year-old with a tragic 40-year history of difficult and erratic behaviour. His life story is that of a deeply wounded man who abuses alcohol and drugs and has a trail of painful relationships resulting in total isolation from his family.
>
> During recovery from alcoholism, he receives psychological counselling. The experience of his abuse returns in soul-crushing power. He is angry and demands financial compensation from the Church for his suffering.

Empathic response to the angry, hostile John is not easy for most people, especially those who believe he is only after money and revenge. He is victimized once again. At the Summit, Cardinal Tagle said, "Beholding Jesus wounded by betrayal and abuse of power, we see the wounds of those hurt by those who should have protected them ... Only by touching the wounds of Jesus did the Apostle Thomas reach faith in the resurrection. Just as the church cannot ignore the suffering of Jesus, neither can it ignore the wounds of the survivors of abuse."

Almost all cases of sexual abuse of minors by clergy are old ones. Like John's case, they have been borne in silence and presented after years of damage. Because of the nature of the psychological damage, the time from abuse to the revelation of the abuse is on average 25 years for males and 18 years for females. Up to 40 percent of survivors have no demonstrated pathology in adulthood. But there is now a wealth of empirical research on the devastating emotional, psychological and physical consequences of childhood sexual abuse, most of it life-long without appropriate treatment. These include feelings of guilt and shame and negative self-image; confusion about sexual norms, standards and identity; profound difficulties with trust and relationships; a sense of helplessness that interferes with the basic pursuit of life goals, including education and employment; depression; anxiety; anger; and suicidal tendencies.[5] There is a small risk of survivors responding by becoming abusers themselves to regain power and control.

In addition to general harms, the sexual exploitation of children and youth by members of the clergy has direct and calamitous effects on faith and spirituality. These were not studied before 2009. Victims conditioned by a combination of Church teaching and myths believed in an all-powerful God. Victims can feel violated and abandoned by God and lose trust in God.[6] Some compare the catastrophic effects of this spiritual abuse to soul murder. Victims can experience despair from confusion about or the loss of God. Beliefs in the Church as a place of holiness and security can be shattered forever. Victims lose the support of a spiritual family, especially in the inability to participate in the liturgical life of the community. Attitudes toward priests are changed profoundly: from revering them to feeling angry at them, compounded by guilt at having caused the abuse and guilt at being angry with a priest. This damage was exacerbated when Church officials failed to believe victims, required a continuation of the secrecy that dominated the abuse, and protected the abuser over victims and their families. Against such a background, healing becomes complex, and being exhorted to pray is insufficient.

Many treatment needs of men and women survivors overlap, as both groups have been forced and seduced into premature sexual activity. Male survivors are more susceptible to internalizing effects; women more to externalizing effects. Girls, influenced by cultural ideals of feminine weakness and vulnerability, understand themselves as victims. Boys, who have absorbed masculine ideals of strength and power, have difficulties accepting themselves as victims. They come to believe they wanted the sex or are gay, which tends to protect the abuser by maintaining secrecy. The vast majority of victims of clergy sexual abuse are boys. They can have difficulty expressing emotions and hold beliefs that they are invulnerable to abuse, that a physical response to offenders means consent and male-to-male activity means homosexuality. They experience shame and feelings of inadequacy for not resisting and have ongoing concerns about their own sexuality.

Psychological counselling is an essential component of treatment, as survivors may have post-traumatic stress disorder (PTSD), depression, anxiety and addictions. The aims of this counselling include giving voice to the trauma and feelings of fear and helping victims to regain trust. Time and emotional commitment are needed for healing. It takes a community to raise a child, to abuse one, and to heal one. We lack appropriate therapists for victims of clergy abuse. Many therapists do not recognize the unique added spiritual harms when the perpetrator is a "man of God." Spiritual healing is key for all people, but particularly for persons of faith. Children believe that the world and God are good, not dangerous and hurtful. Images of God and trust in God are shattered; they lose the consolation of the faith at a time of great need! But pastoral care using religious sources for helping empower people to heal and grow in holiness may be the last thing needed, because it triggers physical, emotional and spiritual trauma with the smell of incense, the sound of church bells, and other symbols. Healing and reconciliation cannot be forced. These are long processes that move at an individual pace. With help, many victims come to some healing, but not reconciliation with God or with the Church.

Because we are one body in Christ, "If one member suffers, all suffer together with it" (1 Corinthians 12:26). While the harm to victims is our first concern, sexual abuse has profound effects on the families of both victims and offenders. Victims' families – both intact families and vulnerable ones, such as those with single parents – suffered guilt over failure to protect their children. Families can experience isolation in such circumstances. As with all whistleblowers, they are often labelled troublemakers for identifying the abuse.[7] It can be difficult for them to afford and access appropriate counselling services, especially if victims turn to anti-social behaviors of all kinds, drugs or suicide. The entire family can be torn apart by the abuse and needs counselling, too. At the 2019 Vatican Summit, Cardinal Cupich of Chicago recognized that "None of the structural elements we enact as a synodal Church, important as they are, can guide us forward faithfully in Christ unless we anchor all our deliberations in the piercing pain of those who have been abused and of the families who have suffered with them."

Parish communities experience grief and anger at the breach of trust and the divisions that grow between supporters of the offending priest and others.[8] Some leave the parish or the Church; others withhold time or financial support. Distrust of any new priest leaves a parish weakened in response. Safe ministry requirements can be onerous; many youth ministry programs may be cancelled or are seen as places of risk instead of being supported enthusiastically. Dioceses are impacted especially when large amounts of money have been paid out in legal settlements.

Non-offending priests and bishops have been badly scarred. We have come a long way in a short time from "priests on pedestals" to "pedophile priests." Those who have done nothing wrong experience shame and stigma. Many have responded by distancing themselves from all activities with children, and avoid physical touch when comfort and support are needed more than ever. Because the focus when the abuse became public was on the offending priest and not on the insensitive and ineffective leadership response, many priests no longer trust their bishop.

Dynamics of abuse

Many disciplines sought to understand why and how this abuse occurs. Society and the media have focused on the individual offenders, the hated and feared pedophiles.[9] Initial research also focused on identifying risk factors in the perpetrators. Sexually abusive relationships may be intimate, personal and secret, but they are not isolated. They exist in virtually all communities and cultures. The harm to one child is not limited to that child, but affects all children and the entire community. It creates fear and distrust and a culture of secrecy. Although it occurs to individuals, it has direct consequences on cultural forces such as children's social and legal status, statutes of limitations, adult sexual immaturity, authoritarianism and clericalism.

In 1984, sociologist David Finkelhor pioneered the first multi-factorial explanation for the sexual abuse of children and youth. He posited that four preconditions are necessary for it to occur: moti-vation to abuse; overcoming of internal inhibitors; overcoming the child or youth's resistance; and overcoming external factors.[10] Each precondition includes personal risk factors, systemic and cultural beliefs and practices, and situational factors that facilitated the abuse. Here we reflect on some Church-specific elements of the preconditions that require deeper investigation.

Motivation to abuse

Identified motivational factors include emotional congruence, whereby some emotional needs are met by the child because of the adult's immature emotional and psychological development; deviant sexual arousal to children that may be related to early developmental experiences; and blockage of healthy relationships, such as through fear of intimacy or physical/social obstruction of access to appropri-ate sexual and emotional partners. Social factors such as notions of sexuality and masculinity also play a role in conditioning.

In the late 1960s and 1970s, research emerged about the emo-tional and sexual immaturity of many priests, which was fostered by the closed clerical culture of seminaries.[11] Difficulties for clergy in communicating their emotional needs, sexuality and masculinity are known.[1] Only with Pope John Paul II's *Pastores Dabo Vobis* in 1992[1] was human development added to the traditional spiritual, intellectual and pastoral pillars of priestly formation.

Most sexual offenders against children and youth in society and in the Church are male. Women abuse physically and emotionally, as institutional abuse and tough nuns in schools have demonstrated. Despite the widespread media use of the term "pedophile priests," the vast majority of clergy offenders are not pedophiles in the strict sense of the term. Pedophiles have a sexual predilection for pre-pubertal children. Research has shown that there are two types of clergy offenders: fixed sexual predators and situational offenders.[1] Fixed sexual predators are a category in the psychiatric literature. They often have narcissistic personality disorder and are psychopaths with no moral sense of what they have done. These are the charismatic offenders with multiple victims, sometimes hundreds of them. Situational offenders are psychologically and psychosexually confused or immature, with a variety of psychological problems. Loneliness and alcohol abuse often trigger their abuse in a single victim or few victims. Most clergy offenders are situational offenders. This raises major questions when it comes to the screening of candidates for the priesthood, their seminary formation and ongoing support of priests after ordination.[1]

While celibacy itself is not a precondition for abusing minors, research has demonstrated that celibate priests have difficulties with emotional intimacy in their relationships with people. Often, friendships with both men and women are highly scrutinized.[1] A theology of sexuality characterized by secrecy, negativity or unattainable idealism has played a role. The meaning and shape of masculinity is an unexplored issue for clergy of the Latin rite who are called to mandatory celibacy. What model of successful male are they to emulate: jock, playboy, successful builder and businessman? Paradoxically, they have roles that are considered feminine, even though all in power in the Church are male. Many men make their work a religion.

Overcoming of internal inhibitors

There must also be an overcoming of strong internal inhibitions to the sexual abuse of children and youth. This can result from such issues as mental illness, alcohol use and the creation of excuses and justifications for the abuse. Social beliefs in patriarchal rights over children have a strong influence. Abusers tend to erase power differences and see victims as "little adults" participating voluntarily in the abuse in a variation on rape-shaming, as in excuses that "he made me do it."

The deeply embedded split between clergy and laity and the special status of the ordained in a theology of priesthood that sets priests above and apart, even as ontologically different, has fostered a sense that priests are above ordinary norms.

Overcoming the child or youth's resistance

Overcoming the resistance of a child or youth to sexual abuse involves the special status of the offender, seduction and desensitization to sex, grooming of victims with gifts, establishing emotional dependence and the use of threats or violence. Victims, conditioned by their religious indoctrination, looked on the priest-abuser with a mixture of awe and fear, producing religious duress. The priest's attitude of superiority elicited trust from his victim. Demands for secrecy, along with sacrilege, blasphemy and threats, were often used.[1]

Overcoming external factors

There must be the opportunity to abuse through planning or taking advantage of opportunity. These require a diminished vigilance in protecting children, such as absent, ill or vulnerable parents, and opportunities for victim and offender to be alone. Parents often enabled the abuse because during the peak times of these offences, priests had almost unlimited access to children and youth, especially boys. Many parents, conditioned to believe in the holiness of the priest, refused to believe their children and even punished them when they revealed the abuse. Some parents who reported the offenses acquiesced to maintaining secrecy.

As the award-winning movie *Spotlight* dramatically showed, police and government officials often privileged the clergy when allegations were made. Church leadership strategies to avoid scandal compromised their duty of protection. Also, clericalism diminished protection in at least three ways.

First, priest abusers and their superiors operated within an enclosed, self-protective clerical culture. Second, priests moved from assignment to assignment without the open process of inquiry, interview and evaluation that was characteristic of many other religious groups as well as professional appointments. Third, a powerful aura of being consecrated surrounded the Catholic priesthood.[1]

The role of moral theology

We begin our investigations searching for insights from moral theology because our response to a moral issue, such as the abuse of the vulnerable, is determined in large part by our perception of the kind of issue we are facing. Our perception has been shaped by what our culture has taught us is acceptable, good and bad. Repentance, reform and renewal begin with the acknowledgement that the issue has moral significance.

Moral theology is the systematic study of the moral life and actions within the Catholic community. It has traditionally focused on moral manuals, specifying rules and norms regarding sins. Theological and pastoral reflection on the moral life, beyond identifying sins, emerged in the pre–Vatican II era and has focused on the positive aspects of the moral life, including conscience, virtue and formation to discipleship.[19]

Moral theology as an independent discipline was created at the end of the 16th century and is historically related to the prior penitential books, which had been developed to prepare seminarians for administering the sacrament of penance. Richard McCormick describes this moral theology as sin-centred, confession-oriented and seminary-controlled.[20] The moral life was one of obedience to the commandments and to the canon law of the Church. Law was the norm of actions and obedience was the highest, some say only, virtue. Because of its focus on the details of sins and laws as written in texts or manuals, this was called the manualist approach to moral theology. It generally involved a deductive process starting with knowledge of exactly what the Church taught about particular, especially sinful issues and acting appropriately. The moral life was understood as a series of individual willed acts with no attention to the direct personal or communal consequences of the acts. This approach to the moral life was developed with little attention to scripture or to virtue ethics or formation of conscience. This is the approach in which priests were formed.

Within this understanding, the problem of abuse was perceived as a sin, a moral lapse that could be confessed and forgiven, and a source of scandal. Knowing this was the theology in which priests were formed helps us understand how they could abuse minors and still believe they had not violated promises of celibacy. It was also the way parents and other laity were taught. Despite their horror and shock at the abuse of their own child, parents and other laity obeyed orders to keep silent about the abuse of their child even when they saw offenders being transferred to unsuspecting new parishes where other children were put at risk. The isolation of individual acts precluded any awareness of the systemic nature of the activities.

From the 1950s on, an evolution in moral theology unfolded.[21] The opening words to Bernard Häring's *The Law of Christ* were clear: the focus of moral theology was not on rules or individual acts of men and women, but on the Lord: "the principle, the norm, the centre, and the goal of Christian moral theology is Christ."[22] Vatican II called for a restoration of the theological focus on the whole of the Christian moral life that integrated moral theology with scripture, spirituality and theology. Moral theology's basic tasks, then, are to provide the right vision for Christian discipleship, to assess perspectives on moral issues, and to present those truths and values that should inform decisions taken in faith.

Ancient Catholic doctrine on the authority and inviolability of personal conscience is clear. However, it was displaced in the 19th and early 20th centuries by magisterial authority, rules and demands for submission. Vatican II restated this primacy of conscience in *Dignitatis Humanae*, which proclaims, "In all his activity a man is bound to follow his conscience in order that he may come to God, the end and purpose of life."[23] Church teaching assumes an informed conscience. This formation comes from scripture, Tradition – especially magisterial or formal Church teaching – experience and science. For generations, following your conscience was reduced to following magisterial teaching to the letter. After the Second World War, the call of European theologians for renewed attention to conscience came from their keen awareness of Catholic participation in atrocities in the war and in concentration camps. They had deep concern that moral theology had fostered obedience to authority and passivity in looking to Rome for answers to difficult questions. Most American theologians resisted this call to renew conscience, preferring the law-and-order approach that they saw as winning the war against evil because it fostered obedience to authority.

Formation of the person to conscience requires openness to the word and call of God, as in Mary's "Let it be with me according to your word" (Luke 1:38) and Jesus' "Not my will but yours be done" (Luke 22:42). Conscience is a "knowing together." While it is deeply personal, it is formed in community. It is relational and responsible, avoids self-centredness and strives to live a life oriented to God and virtues. Where and how do Catholics inform their conscience? It is rarely preached about. A 2017 survey indicated that they inform their conscience by private prayer and the opinions of family and friends, rather than from Church sources such as their priest, the *Catechism of the Catholic Church* or papal statements.

The abuse crisis demonstrates the urgent need to recover conscience and move from a rule and duty ethic of obedience to virtue ethics. Virtue focuses on questions of who we are and who we ought to become. Crucially, it recognizes that our decisions and actions reflect and shape our character. In the spiritual sense, attention to virtue focuses on forming and supporting hearts and minds. The *Catechism of the Catholic Church* states that "A virtue is an habitual and firm disposition to do the good. It allows the person not only to perform good acts, but to give the best of [her]self. The virtuous person tends toward the good with all his sensory and spiritual powers; [s]he pursues the good and chooses it in concrete actions" (no. 1803). The notion of virtue and its importance in the moral life is central to Church teaching. Virtue ethics rightly realizes the ways that we are related to God, others and all of creation.[24] Individuals become virtuous with and through the inspiration and guidance of others. In such a view, rules and laws are not thrown away; rather, they are moved from the human tendency to absolutize them and make things black or white, to a form of guidance or wisdom from past experience that helps a person discern the right or good action in a particular situation. Conscience, built upon strong virtues and the will to do good, becomes an instrument of discernment rather than an application of the law.

The theological virtues of faith, hope and charity (love) are infused by God's grace into the soul of the faithful. The greatest desire, to please God, as lived out in these three theological virtues is essential for creating a culture in which all members have a desire and ongoing commitment to do good. Love, mercy, reconciliation and hope characterize our understanding of Christian virtue ethics.[25] Ultimately, it is the theological virtue of charity/love that must be paramount, as charity is the animator and binder of all of the other virtues. Any reform and renewal in the Church must be animated by love: love of God and love of others. This love, which mirrors the love in the Trinity, involves mutual relationships and a constantly interactive communion. It is from Jesus, whose love is total giving of oneself without need for return or mutuality. This love leads to communal healing and internal dispositions that form us as disciples. In addition to a restoration of virtue ethics, renewed attention to Catholic social justice ethics, which began with *Rerum Novarum* in 1891,[26] can restore a more just and personalist focus of responsibilities and relationship to our moral thinking.

Situating the moral approach

Moral theologian Norbert Rigali notes the failure to address

> the harm the priest does to the child – a crime of one person
> against another and against the social order; a matter calling
> for justice for the victim, punishment and rehabilitation for
> the perpetrator, and the redress of the community life. What
> is missing from the clerical perception and is of the essence of
> the parental perception is the presence of *the other* – the per-
> son affected by the doer and of the community social order.[27]

Moral theology without virtue ethics and a sense of justice focused
only on the sin and the sinner; it lacked a relational understanding of
sin and its consequences.[28]

Classic psychological research on gender difference and moral
reasoning suggests that women presented with moral conflicts tend to
focus on details about relationships and ways to protect all, while men
tend to identify rules that apply to the situation and then act according
to the dominant rule.[29] Some writers distinguished these as an ethic
of care in contrast to an ethic of justice. These differences are in part
socially determined. They are not intended to be sexist judgments. Of
course, some men choose care approaches and some women choose
justice approaches, but general differences are important to consider.
In a patriarchal system, such as the Church, females are subordinated
to males and the relational wisdom of women is lost from discernment
and decision making.[30]

Christian feminist ethics criticizes human relationships of power,
violence, and the theological justification of the inferiority of women
to men; challenges the male–female states as polar opposites; and
empowers the responsibility of all for fostering the common good.[31]
Catholic feminist theology has crucial insights that are necessary for
the real, active participation of all in the life and work of the Church.
Catholic feminist ethics, rooted in the experience of women in the

world and in the Church, commits to equal personal dignity, equal mutual respect and equal social power for men and women.[32]

Sadly, the review of the history of the clergy abuse crisis demonstrated ongoing resistance to reform of both Catholic moral theology and the theology of sexuality which was exacerbated by the 2019 essay by former Pope Benedict XVI. As Cardinal Ratzinger, a member of the Congregation for the Doctrine of the Faith, he barred Fr. Charles Curran from teaching theology at the Catholic University of America and investigated and condemned theologian Sister Margaret Farley's book *Just Love: A Framework for Christian Sexual Ethics*.[33]

The lack of a theology of children

While children are considered gifts of God to parents, the Church has no theology of children or explicit obligation of protection.[34] Jesus' interaction with children was profoundly counter-cultural.[35] When the apostles tried to shoo them away, Jesus "called for them" (Luke 18:16), "took them up in his arms, laid his hands on them, and blessed them" (Mark 10:16).

Cultures have strong ideas and beliefs about children. Patriarchal cultures have seen children as property, like slaves. Children are to be seen but not heard, and completely subject to parental authority. Tragically, the Church's failure to be counter-cultural, as Jesus was, has contributed to their abuse. Children have no power and are dependent on others. Many priests have little or no experience in caring for children. They are called "Father" but never "Dad," and miss the important psychological impact of fathering in male maturation. Clearly, the abuse crisis raises challenges for disciples of Christ to reflect on a theology of children and childhood appropriate for our time. This includes education to safe touch and the promotion of safe ministry environments. But it goes far beyond these, and includes protecting youth from all forces of corruption in our society and fostering their human and spiritual development as disciples for today and tomorrow.

Church-specific beliefs and practices in the dynamics of clergy sexual abuse

The dynamics identify many Church factors, both beliefs and practices, in need of further study. In this chapter we examined briefly the role of moral theology and the lack of a counter-cultural theology of children and childhood. The following chapters will reflect on differing diagnoses of the fundamental pathology; the role of silence, denial and avoidance of scandal; and the abuse of power and authority.

Pastoral pause and prayer

> ➤ How do you feel when you hear stories of the sexual abuse of children and youth by "men of God"?
> ➤ Have you had any direct experience in accompanying victims or survivors?
> ➤ What are your thoughts about Church-specific factors in the dynamics that fostered abuse?
> ➤ Does the Church assist you in forming your conscience in moral matters?
> ➤ What is the cry of your heart when you bring this issue to the Lord?

Chapter 3

Diagnostic Disagreements and Fractures in the Body of Christ

"I am the way, and the truth, and the life." (John 14:6)

Introduction

Jesus was sent to restore the union between God and all creation and to show the way to the reign of God's love, justice and compassion in his words and witness. Jesus himself is the way to the Father and salvation. At the beginning of his public ministry Jesus returns home to Nazareth. There, in the synagogue, he reads from the prophet Isaiah: "'The Spirit of the Lord is upon me, because he has anointed me to bring good news to the poor....' Today this scripture has been fulfilled in your hearing." At first, he wins approval, but then some in the crowd begin to question the legitimacy of this claim from the son of Joseph. When Jesus replies that "no prophet is accepted in the prophet's hometown," this enrages everyone and they "drove him out of town," intending to kill him (Luke 4:16-30).

Throughout his ministry, Jesus faced constant challenges from those who had different ideas about the "right way" to be a child of God. Some question why his disciples did not wash their hands before eating (Mark 7:1-9); others criticize that he would eat with sinners and tax collectors (Mark 2:16). Indeed, he proclaimed, "Do you think that I have come to bring peace to the earth? No, I tell you, but rather division!" (Luke 12:51). He predicted that his message, meant to unite all, would divide families and communities. The division is not created by Jesus, but is a natural outcome of listeners making different decisions about whether and how to follow him. Tragically, the lived experience of the Church is that of much division and dissension about how to be a disciple. Even in the second and third centuries there were debates about the requirement for circumcision. The great epiphany proclamation that "the Gentiles have become fellow heirs, members of the same body, and sharers in the promise in Christ Jesus through the gospel" (Ephesians 3:5-6) was a source of contention, resulting in early fractures to the Body of Christ.

The effectiveness of any prescription depends on an accurate diagnosis of the pathology. After a medical history is taken and a physical exam is performed, physicians must decide on which investigations to pursue toward the diagnosis. Laboratory blood analysis, biopsies, x-rays and scans allow us to go deeper into the mysteries of the body. To focus investigations, there is an initial judgment of the nature of the sickness. For example, trauma, infection, cancer and genetic diseases each have different mechanisms of disease that must be taken into account. The approach to medical investigation can differ significantly, depending on whether the doctor's focus is that of a family doctor, a medical specialist or a surgeon. Legitimate differences about a diagnosis can help challenge biases of perspective and experience. However, significant problems arise in recommending appropriate treatment when the diagnosis of the fundamental pathology differs radically and there are arguments about who is right.

It is clear is that there is an urgent need to make the correct diagnosis of this crisis for the healing of the bruised and fractured Body of Christ. In chapter 1, the history of clergy sexual abuse demonstrated long-standing signs and symptoms of spiritual and ecclesial pathology. This is first of all obvious in the totally inadequate and insensitive response to the harm done to children and youth. It is also manifested in a persistent focus on individual priests and, recently, bishops and cardinals, and the ongoing failure to identify and address the deep systemic and cultural factors operative in the abuse of individuals and in Church leadership response. Chapter 2 revealed that as the profound harms of the sexual abuse of minors were becoming understood and acknowledged in the 1970s and 1980s in North America, many disciplines sought to understand why and how the sexual abuse of vulnerable and dependent children and youth occurs. The brief review of the dynamics of the sexual abuse of minors by clergy made clear the importance of systemic and cultural factors, including beliefs, practices, relationships and organization. There, the role of moral theology and the crucial need to focus on conscience formation and virtues necessary for the discernment required to go forward in "the mind of Christ" for clergy and laity alike were identified. We explored Jesus' counter-cultural understandings of children in his rejection of patriarchal beliefs and our lack of a theology of children.

The goals of this chapter are to review the scholarly theological and empirical analysis of cultural and systemic pathology and ecclesial sin in the crisis. The insights from some single-issue diagnoses will be examined, with particular attention to the role of the Catholic theology of sexuality and sexual morality in shaping the crisis. Finally, we will address the significant challenges presented to conversion, reform and healing from polarizing divisions and incompatible diagnoses.

Systemic diagnosis and ecclesial sin

The history of clergy sexual abuse clearly shows that the essential characteristics of Church leadership response to the crisis manifested in these pathologies – in the United States, Canada, Ireland, elsewhere in the global North, and in Australia – transcend national and cultural differences. The response has been characterized by secrecy, denial, insensitivity to victims and the need to minimize harm, and protection of offenders and institution image to avoid scandal. The history reveals an implicit diagnosis supported by almost all Church leadership, those most embedded in Church culture and organization.

These understand the Church as *the perfect society*, essentially in good health but wounded by the sins and failings of individual priests and bishops and targeted by the media. Treatment here is simply to weed out "bad apples" from the priesthood and require adherence to rules and updated procedures, protocols and audits to safeguard children. This understanding is problematic because ecclesial, institutional and organizational sin is rejected as incompatible with ecclesial perfection and irrelevant in the clergy abuse crisis.

A different diagnosis is supported by many scholars from diverse fields, history, the dynamics of abuse, and insights from as far back as the 1990 Commission report from the Archdiocese of St. John's, Newfoundland. That report concluded that there is no single cause for the crisis. It identified systemic and cultural issues manifested in the crisis that required further study: these included abuse of power, the education of clergy and laity, sexuality, support for priests, and the Church's management approach to avoidance of scandal. This diagnosis is totally compatible with empirical research, which requires us to "view the phenomenon in the universe of the organization as a breakdown of the institution, disregarded or facilitated by the underlying organizational structure in which the harm occurred. It is important to look at child sexual abuse within the Catholic Church as an individual problem enabled by the organization."[1] In other terms, "Essentially, it is the organization's culture, values, policies, and system of rewards and sanctions in combination with the individual dynamics of the seminarian or priest, as well as situational factors, that best account for sexual misconduct among priests."[2] The organizational context for the crisis has been examined from many theological disciplines, but also from psychology, sociology, law and organizational studies.[3]

Marie Keenan's masterful review concludes that in contrast to the widespread belief that public moral failure of organizations and institutions is the result of individual members failing to obey rules, researchers have found that "poor and undesirable outcomes … are socially organized phenomena that are produced by the connections between the institutional environment (which also includes the social context, including political, technological, economic, demographic, legal, cultural, and ecological aspects), the particular organizational characteristics and individual cognition."[4] Social science analyses have positioned this as a crisis of trust – not just in individuals, but a "structural betrayal of trust."[5] The loss of trust has been caused by misunderstanding the nature and use of authority, power and privilege, the unwillingness to learn from scholarly disciplines, and a lack of empathy and compassion in relating to the ordinary experiences of human beings.

As we saw in chapter 1, Fr. Thomas Doyle, who has studied this issue since its emergence, has observed that "In spite of the number of recorded clergy abuse cases throughout the world, the official Church refuses or is unable to make any connection between the clerical abuse crisis and the internal structural dynamics of the Catholic Church."[6] At the 2019 Summit, Cardinal Tagle publicly acknowledged some of these links: "The sexual abuse of minors and vulnerable adults in the Church reveals a complex web of interconnected factors including: psychopathology, sinful moral decisions, social environments that enable abuse to happen, and often inadequate or plainly harmful institutional and pastoral responses, or a lack of response." The systemic and cultural diagnosis recognizes the critical importance not just of personal sin but also of ecclesial sin. It is compatible with the belief that the Church is both holy and sinful. It is holy in its members and holy in its structures, but at the same time sinful in its members and structures.[7]

The significance of single-issue diagnosis

Despite the identification of this complex systemic and cultural diagnosis, made by scholars in theology and many empirical disciplines, history clearly shows a refusal or inability of Church leaders and many laity to accept this diagnosis. In trying to make sense of the crisis, many have focused on specific issues as *the* cause. It is understandable that we seek a specific simple diagnosis for a health problem, particularly if it has a quick fix in a pill or procedure. In contrast, a serious, complex diagnosis requiring a number of different investigations and interventions and, most difficult of all, a change in lifestyle is difficult to accept. In clinging to a single-issue diagnosis, many forget the old story of three blind men who have never heard of elephants and what happens when they meet one. Each man grabs a different part of the elephant: one the writhing and snorting trunk; another, the thin and whipping tail; and the third, a massive and unyielding leg. Each is holding an elephant and has real physical contact. Each accurately describes what they experience as elephant, but all are incomplete in their understanding of the wonderful living animal with many different parts. In the same way, each of the individual issues identified contains important insights into the complexity of making the correct diagnosis, but none on its own describes the situation of clergy sexual abuse.

It is for some a crisis of a general *infidelity* and of *disobedience* to authority. It is about liberal seminary professors, priests who question Tradition and formal magisterial teaching, and theologians who encourage a "culture of dissent."[8]

Feminist analysis sees *patriarchy*, a social system in which the male role as primary authority is a central feature, as the cause of the crisis. In a patriarchal system, females are subordinate to males; as was clear in the dynamics of the sexual abuse of minors described in chapter 2, the relational wisdom of women is lost from moral discernment and decision making. Feminist theology has insights that are crucial for the real, active participation of all in the life and work of the Church. Specifically, feminist theology advocates for the vulnerable, whose needs are understood to be above the needs of the privileged and powerful. Because repentance of sin does not guarantee the strength to resist that sin in future, feminist approaches don't just help empower individuals, but explore ways to counter systemic and cultural forces that create vulnerability and deny their exploitation.

So, feminist theology and ethics demand critical analysis of systemic and cultural factors that create vulnerability; they understand the importance of medical and social science research in a critically constructive analysis.[10]

The role of the Catholic theology of sexuality and sexual morality

For a substantial number of Catholics, this is a crisis of *sexuality*. The urgent need for open and honest discussion of sexual needs, intimacy, masculinity and celibacy has been clearly identified by therapists: "Catholic moral theologians need to develop a developmentally and scientifically appropriate narrative of human sexuality for parishioners and clergy. Unless this is forthcoming we will continue to see perverse sexual enactments among a subset of the clergy...."[11] There are links between the inadequacy of our moral theology, which was reviewed in chapter 2, Catholic sexual morality, and a theology of sexuality. As Fr. Norbert Rigali has noted in studying the abuse crisis, "The moral perceptions and discernments of Church authorities with regard to the sexual abuse of children by priests, then, reflected not only moral theology's inadequate conception of Christian morality and of sin but also the discipline's inadequate treatment of human sexuality and the Church's lack of an adequate theology of human sexuality."[12]

However, there are at least four different diagnoses of this crisis of *sexuality*. The first is that despite the long-standing history of the issue, the Church has not been aggressive enough on enforcing sexual teachings and keeping all sexual activity within marriage. The sexual liberation of the 1960s and 1970s rejected that, so the prescription is clearly to hold all to chastity, teach more forcefully on every aspect of human sexuality, and enforce the teaching. This is the view of former Pope Benedict, who often spoke of the important influence of St. Augustine on his own understanding of human sexuality. Augustine was suspicious of sexual desire and sexual acts. Theologian Cristina Traina concludes that "Augustine's belief that even 'good' marital sex, which is only redeemed by procreation, ought to be hidden away ... has probably contributed more than anything else to the impression that our sexuality is essentially private."[13] This suspicion and private understanding contributed to the secrecy dominating sexual abuse.

Others believe a *repressive approach to sexuality* and an *outdated anthropology* contributed to the tolerance of secretive and distorted sexual activity.[14] Their prescription is a renewed theology of sexuality that is not developed solely by old, celibate, powerful males but includes all – clergy, lay, celibate, married, single and those in committed relationships – in the dialogue.[15] Tragically, the history of Catholic moral theologians who have been silenced because of attempts to renew sexual teaching is sobering.

Yet another interpretation sees *mandatory celibacy*, with its aura of the supernatural, suggesting a holier state of priests than of laity and raising impossible expectations for behaviour and relationships. The loneliness and sexual immaturity in the lives of many priests is problematic.

Since the disgrace of Cardinal McCarrick, many have increased their focus on *homosexuality* as the cause of the crisis. This is despite all the evidence that mature homosexuals are no more likely to offend against a minor than is a mature heterosexual. There are a high number of homosexuals in the clergy, but correlation is not causation. Homosexuality is a cause of great anguish for many and great anger for others. Scapegoating homosexuality highlights the urgent need to address the issue in a renewed theology of sexuality. Traditionalists use a hierarchical approach to the issue and privilege magisterial teaching, which has declared that homosexual acts are "intrinsically disordered." Theologians attempting a revision of sexual theology take magisterial teaching seriously, but assess it in light of scripture, reason and experience. Modern understandings of homosexuality as a disposition, not a moral choice, and the witness of loving committed homosexual relationships demand a new way of thinking and judging in this area.

Bernard Häring recognized that an adequate moral theology of human sexuality required an authentic theology of sexuality. Catholic sexual morality's absolute, proscriptive norms privilege the biological function of the sexual act over its personal relational and spiritual meanings. The *Catechism of the Catholic Church* states, "Sexuality affects all aspects of the human person in the unity of his body and soul. It especially concerns affectivity, the capacity to love and to procreate, and in a more general way the aptitude for forming bonds of communion with others" (no. 2332). Modern society is awash in sexual exploitation and violence, especially toward women and children. While society expresses public horror at the sexual abuse of children and youth, pornography – including child pornography – is rampant, and TV and movies are replete with sexual manipulation and exploitation. Prostitution and human trafficking are worldwide phenomena. It is precisely in this area of sexual morality that modern society is desperately in need of the gospel witness of justice, compassion, tenderness and mercy, and that the Church has lost credibility.

On the one hand, Catholics often experience the preaching of an impossibly ideal set of magisterial statements on marriage and sexuality. On the other hand, many Catholics have a general perception of sexuality as "dirty," secret and sinful. Catholics influenced by the Second Vatican Council experienced new and powerful teaching on the gift of human sexuality, especially in the married state. But for most, Catholic moral teaching has been dominated by rules and prohibitions regarding sexual and reproductive issues. As a result, many Catholics have experienced the Church as laying heavy burdens in the area of sexual behaviour: for example, the mother of seven with a husband who demands sex and who can't use artificial contraception; frowning upon the use of condoms in preventing HIV in Africa; and infertile couples desperately desiring children but having limited approval to use modern medical technology to assist them. In a deep sense, teachings about sexuality and forgiveness for sexual sins are experienced as issues of power and control, not as the reconciling mercy of Jesus Christ. There are also sharp inconsistencies between Catholic social ethics, which is principle oriented, relational focused, dynamic, developmental and inductive, and Catholic sexual ethics, which is law oriented, legalistic, act focused, static and deductive.[16] This fosters confusion.

For all of Catholicism's focus on sexual morality, Jesus himself had little to say about it. Arguably, the most compelling story that comes to mind when we think of the gospel and sexuality is that of Jesus and the woman taken in adultery (John 8:3-11). There, it is Jesus' enormous sensitivity and compassion to the woman that impresses and comforts. Even in affirming the Old Testament prohibition on divorce (Matthew 19:3-9), Jesus grants an exception in the case of sexual immorality, demonstrating his understanding of the gap between the ideal and lived human experience. In general, the Christian scriptures demonstrate considerable ambiguity and contradiction regarding human bodies and sexuality.

A crisis of obedience and a crisis of sexuality are linked in the story of Pope Paul VI's 1968 Encyclical *Humanae Vitae*, On the Regulation of Birth.[17] It transformed Catholics' relationship of obedience to Church authority so that today, two thirds of American Catholics say they should rely on their own authority in matters of sexuality. The idea that sex could be an act of love and an essential aspect of marriage did not get much attention before the Second Vatican Council. Pope John XXIII called the Council to prepare the Church for the modern world. One major event requiring an urgent response was the development of birth control in 1960. The Pope created a small expert Pontifical Commission for the Study of Population, Family and Births. Before it met for the first time, Pope John died. His successor, Pope Paul VI, confirmed the Commission and added 50 more members, many of them high-ranking clerics. He removed birth control from the Council agenda, indicating that it would be dealt with by the Commission. However, he rejected the Majority Report, which affirmed that "In resolving the ... problem of responsible parenthood and the appropriate determination of the size of the family … the objective criteria are to be applied by the couples, acting from a rightly informed conscience and according to their concrete situation."[18] The failure of reception of *Humanae Vitae* has had serious corrosive effects on Catholics and the inclusion of Church teaching in their formation of conscience ever since.

Pope John Paul II responded to what he saw as the pastoral and catechetical failure of *Humanae Vitae* in a series of lectures that form *The Theology of the Body: Human Love in the Divine Plan*.[19] This work has met with some enthusiasm, especially from some younger Catholics who are searching for a story of what authentic sexual relationships might look like in our promiscuous society. However, there are many concerns about the adequacy of his approach and analysis. Reducing a theology of the body to idealized sexuality and limiting sexuality to intercourse is fundamentally flawed. In the Pope's formulations, human sexuality is observed from a distance. This is not unreasonable coming from an elderly celibate cleric, but is totally inadequate for the full human experience.

The challenges of different and polarizing diagnosis

"I ask not only on behalf of these, but also on behalf of those who will believe in me through their word, that they may all be one. As you, Father, are in me and I am in you, may they also be in us, so that the world may believe that you have sent me."
(John 17:20-21)

The traditional marks of the Church are that it is one, holy, catholic and apostolic. Unity is the first mark. There are and always have been differences of opinion about how to be a disciple and a Church in the world. However, "The Church's unity is that of a communion, a unity of difference that witnesses to the catholic dimension of God's grace which is neither divisive nor oppressive but gathers up genuine difference in an inclusive wholeness."[20] In his closing remarks at the 2019

Summit, Pope Francis noted that "To achieve that goal [healing], the church must rise above the ideological disputes ... that often exploit, for various interests, the very tragedy experienced by little ones." In the face of the pain and suffering of victims and of the entire Body of Christ, liberal and conservative forces taking advantage of the situation to promote their own agenda is a manifestation of the disease of disunity. The situation is reminiscent of looting on the field of battle for personal gain, or argument over who has the proper vision to reorganize the deck chairs while the barque of Peter is going down!

Recognizing that pastoral concerns about a whole range of issues – including liturgy, religious education and adult catechesis, the loss of vocations and decline of religious participation, especially among the young – were not being addressed due to the increasing polarization among individuals and groups in the Church, Cardinal Joseph Bernardin of Chicago created the Catholic Common Ground Initiative in 1996. He made clear that the invitation

> should not be limited to those who agree in every respect on orientation for the church, but encompass all – whether centrists, moderates, liberals, radicals, conservatives, or neo-conservatives – who are willing to reaffirm basic truths and to pursue their disagreements in renewed spirit of dialogue. Chief among those truths is that our discussion must be accountable to the Catholic tradition and to the Spirit-filled living church that brings to us the revelation of God in Jesus.[21]

Tragically, a movement to restore unity to a fractured Church received very negative reaction from four cardinals, including Boston's Bernard Law and Philadelphia's Anthony Bevilacqua, and a number of bishops because of concerns about diminishing magisterial authority and fostering dissent. Cardinal Law's mismanagement of the crisis and Cardinal Bevilacqua's death before testifying at a grand jury on the issue and on recent allegations of abuse provoke questions regarding their motivations and approach.

Polarizing divisions are more than legitimate differences arising from time, place and culture. Polarization is also different from conflict, which can gather people to resolve and emphasize what they have in common. Polarization is about opposing and irreconcilable beliefs and the organization of all life around the belief. The poles identify themselves against each other and judge right or wrong, holy or sinful according to the party line, not "the mind of Christ." These often vicious divisions in the Church are themselves a pathology in need of healing. They occur throughout the Church but are most evident in the Church in the United States. Universities, lay groups and Church leaders present different diagnoses. Even if it was feasible, restoration to a time when the Church was wealthy and powerful and dominated Western society and culture, including the decisions and actions of Christians, would return to a culture that fostered sexual abuse of the vulnerable. Others want to overly democratize the Church. This polarization is itself sinful disunity, fracturing the Body of Christ and weakening its ability to heal.

Pastoral pause and prayer

> - What are your thoughts on the root causes of the clergy sexual abuse crisis? After reflecting on this chapter, do you have new insights on causes of the crisis?
> - Have you experienced polarizing divisions in your family or faith community about faith or the clergy sexual abuse crisis?
> - How significant for you is the issue of the Church's theology of sexuality and sexual morality?
> - What are your suggestions for healing the divisions and fractures?

Chapter 4

Morally Mute: The Corruption of Silence and Denial

In the beginning was the Word, and the Word was with God, and the Word was God. (John 1:1-3)

Introduction

Throughout his ministry, Jesus saw and responded to oppression and falsehood. He relentlessly spoke out and named the issues directly. In speaking truth to power, he was not only speaking out against injustice and oppression, but was challenging the silence and denial that allow the injustice to develop and endure. He declares that "The truth will make you free" (John 8:32). Jesus said to some Pharisees, "If you were blind, you would not have sin. But now that you say, 'We see,' your sin remains" (John 9:40-41). He reminds us that when we claim to "see," an essential moral responsibility follows.

Jesus recognizes the human desire to protect and promote our egos and status. He boldly describes the cost that follows when this desire overwhelms obligations and duties to others when he says of leaders, "They do all their deeds to be seen by others; for they make their phylacteries broad and their fringes long. They love to have the place of honour at banquets and the best seats in the synagogues, and to be greeted with respect in the marketplaces, and to have people call them rabbi" (Matthew 23:5), and "... do whatever [the scribes and the

Pharisees] teach you and follow it; but do not do as they do, for they do not practice what they preach. They tie up heavy burdens, hard to bear, and lay them on the shoulders of others; but they themselves are unwilling to lift a finger to move them" (Matthew 23:1-3).

During his ministry, Jesus experienced denial from friends and enemies alike who challenged his identity and mission. When he tried to speak to his disciples about his upcoming Passion and death, "they did not understand what he was saying and were afraid to ask him" (Mark 9:31-32). He felt the pain of Peter, the rock on whom he later built the Church, denying even knowing him when things became dangerous.

Denial is a natural defense mechanism that regularly surfaces in the context of health care. Patients ignore symptoms, hoping they will just go away. Both patients and doctors use euphemisms or indirect language, rather than engage in difficult discussions about complicated and terminal illness.[1] After death, many will say things such as the patient "passed" rather than "died." Denying the diagnosis of serious and life-threatening or life-altering disease for ourselves or our loved ones can actually help us when we begin to cope with the realities of illness, dependence and dying. Denial can allow us to pace our response gradually. However, persistent denial in the face of serious threats to life and health becomes a pathology all its own. In pediatric practice, I was often involved with dysfunctional families who were unable to face the reality of difficult situations or talk about any of their problems.

In the chapter 1 history of clergy sexual abuse of minors and the chapter 2 review of the dynamics of that abuse, silence and denial dominate. They are characteristic responses at both the level of individual victims and the systemic and global level. In the history of the Church, we find examples of the Church's silence and denial of tragedies: for example, Pope Pius XII's failure to speak out about atrocities in the Holocaust. Fr. Donald Cozzens has said that "what really scandalizes countless numbers of the faithful is the church's readiness – tragically exemplified in recent decades by its response to the sexual misconduct cases involving a significant number of priests and bishops – to deny and minimize the depth, scope, and pastoral implications of issues that cry out for analysis and action."[2]

My goals in this chapter are to assist the Church in acknowledging the crucial role of silence, denial and cover-up in the sexual abuse crisis. We will review insights about silence and denial from sociology, psychology and organizational management studies and assess some Church-specific factors that foster silence and denial. Finally, I propose a new commitment to meaningful, inclusive and courageous dialogue in the Church.

The role of silence and denial in the crisis

Understanding silence and denial is crucially important in understanding sexual abuse, particularly sexual abuse of children and youth by clergy and the Church's insensitive and inadequate response. Silence and denial are intimately related. It has been said that "Indeed, the most public form of denial is silence."[3]

As seen in chapter 2, secrecy and silence were essential components in the abuse of individual victims. Silence was forced on them, even by threats of physical and spiritual consequences to them and their families. The maintenance of silence to avoid scandal, narrowly understood as reputational loss, was imposed on all who revealed the abuse. Scandal in the biblical sense of creating an obstacle for others in their search for God was ignored.[4] A persistent focus on individual perpetrators, the "bad apples" diagnosis, and leadership denial of the deeper systemic and cultural factors that facilitated the abuse and inadequate leadership response prolonged and deepened the harms.

The responses not only failed to care for and protect children but led to outright failure to comply with established canons and relevant law. There is "evidence that Catholic bishops, with very few exceptions, had not only protected the abusers, but in the process had also breached the procedures of both canon and civil law."[5] At the 2019 Summit, we heard Cardinal Marx openly acknowledge that

> Files that could have documented the terrible deeds and named those responsible were destroyed, or not even created. Instead of the perpetrators, the victims were regulated and silence imposed on them. The stipulated procedures and processes for the prosecution of offences were deliberately not complied with, but instead cancelled or overridden. The rights of victims were effectively trampled underfoot.

Recall from the history in chapter 1 that revelations of clergy sexual abuse did not arise as a result of internal examination of conscience from Church leadership in light of increased social understanding of the harms of the sexual abuse of minors in the 1970s and 1980s. The revelations were forced by cases in criminal and civil law and from the work of investigative journalists. There has been criticism from many Church leaders about media bias in covering this issue. At the Summit, surprisingly, Pope Francis thanked journalists for their role in uncovering the abuse. Journalist Valentina Alazraki stated that "the more you cover up … fail to inform the mass media and thus, the faithful and public opinion, the greater the scandal will be." Drawing on a medical metaphor, she noted, "If someone has a tumour, it is not cured by hiding it from one's family or friends; silence will not make it heal; in the end it will be the most highly recommended treatments that will prevent metastasis and lead to healing."

Persistent denial of the significance of the underlying systemic and cultural factors in this crisis, in light of experience and scholarly research, has become pathological denial. This denial causes ongoing pain and suffering and presents a major impediment to healing. Diagnosing the reasons for the ongoing denial becomes itself a crucial component of any effective prescription for healing and renewal.

Insights from empirical studies on silence and denial in organizational moral failure

Silence and denial have been studied in social psychology, political science, communication science and philosophy.[6] Denial is a powerful and pervasive psychological and sociological reality. It is an unconscious defense mechanism for coping with fear, guilt, anxiety and a wide range of disturbing realities in personal life and in social and political life. There are both psychological and sociological forces at work in denial.

Psychological studies show that denial stems from an individual or institutional need to avoid pain or trauma because some things are just "too terrible for words."[7] There is a far-ranging and robust literature on silence and denial in ordinary life in painful situations, as experienced by abuse survivors and family members of alcoholics. There is also a haunting history of social and political denial in situations such as the Holocaust. Much denial also comes simply from fear and embarrassment.

Silence is not merely the lack of speech. The sounds of silence can be a powerful force for good or evil. Because silence requires listeners, the sociology of silence and denial studies the importance of social relations (hierarchy) and social situations (public/private). It recognizes that "as the quintessential public manifestation of denial, conspiracies of silence are clearly socially patterned."[8] This patterning teaches us the bounds of acceptable discourse and the rules of denial. It has been said that "The best way to disrupt moral behavior is not to discuss it and not to discuss not discussing it."[9] Denial requires a deliberate effort not to notice – and especially not to notice serious issues. Denial requires a sensory shutdown as we develop a blind spot or turn a deaf ear to painful topics. We try to avoid the elephant in the room. In society, we learn what to ignore through unwritten rules of irrelevance, taboos (such as the "blue wall" describing silence in police departments about colleague wrongdoing), and the use of euphemisms to soften the power of critique.

The politics of silence and denial are also important. The political dimension demands attention to power in access to information (confidentiality); controlling the scope of others' attention and determining what we can talk about – controlling the agenda; controlling access to information and to its dissemination (such as gag orders; settlements with non-disclosure clauses). Institutionalized prohibitions foster silence and denial by controlling the focus of attention, the scope of the discourse and the power to deny the act of denial. There is a cost to breaking the silence. Painful accounts of the cost to whistleblowers are well known.[10] Bystanders and enablers of silence and denial in the face of wrongdoing compound the painful consequences.

Organizational studies

Organizational and management studies consider issues relating to power, culture and practices that contribute to the moral/ethical life of an organization.[11] This research is understood as "practical theology" that seeks to understand and influence the good in institutions and organizations.[12] The sexual abuse crisis in the Catholic Church is identified as an example of institutional moral failure with lessons for secular organizations.[13] Insofar as the Church is an organization, these secular studies can aid the Church in better understanding the role of silence and denial in this crisis.

Organizations use mechanisms such as mission and value statements and codes of ethics and conduct to promote an ethical/moral culture. However, codes of ethics have become "an institutionalized practice that itself confers a cognitive form of legitimacy to the organization and further distances the codes from their moral foundation."[14] While the values and code of ethics may be framed on the walls and website, little attention may be given to creating an organizational culture that encourages following proclaimed values and living by what codes propose as ethical behaviour.

In addition to psychology and sociology, organizational management studies have pursued the issues of secrecy and denial. Highly publicized public moral failures of trusted organizations and institutions[15] are the subject of considerable research. Media such as movies portray these stories as well: examples include *All the President's Men* on the Watergate scandal, *Silkwood* on nuclear facility safety, and *Spotlight* on the clergy sexual abuse crisis. Silence in the presence of wrongdoing is central to all examples of organizational moral failure.

Research by Elizabeth Morrison and Frances Milliken shows that when an organization is characterized by a culture of silence, "this is less a product of multiple, unconnected individual choices and more a product of forces within the organization – and forces stemming from management – that systematically reinforce silence."[16] They have identified forces fostering organizational silence in an analytic framework that includes management characteristics and beliefs, management structures, policies and practices of decision making, and employee factors.

Significant management factors include a distant and unapproachable management and a high level of dissimilarity between management and others in the organization. This dissimilarity includes gender, race, ethnicity and age, as well as educational background and tenure in position. The more homogeneous the management team, the longer they have been in power together, the more cohesive they are likely to be, and the more threatened by dissent. High vertical differentiation in an organization reinforces silence-creating beliefs and practices. Managerial beliefs that characterize employees as self-interested and untrustworthy play an important role.

Leaders are critical in creating the culture of an organization.[17] Leaders have both structural/hierarchical power related to authority and position as well as prestige power because of their role in the organization. However, the influence of power and self-focus in leaders can adversely affect their ability to respond to moral issues because they tend to be overconfident, fail to appreciate input from others and misread situations as a result.[18] Addiction to power and denial are connected: leaders will use defense mechanisms such as hiding, ignoring or changing information to avoid embarrassing, threatening or painful situations. These contribute to an inability to learn from studies on effective responses to public moral failure, which include admitting incompetence, ceding control and demonstrating attitudes and practices that are clearly new.

Management structures, policies and practices that centralize decision making and avoid or reject negative feedback are powerful in silencing employees. Psychological studies suggest that "hierarchical models of accountability by their very nature foster mechanisms of denial."[19]

Morrison and Milliken also identified relevant employee factors in silence and denial. These include similarity in background; strengthening the differences between employees and management; and policies and practices that adversely affect employees' interactions, communication, and opportunities for collective sense-making when they experience a serious discrepancy between organizational and management behaviour and espoused values – such as in a public moral failure. This discrepancy evokes anger in personal and professional life, individually and collectively, and the need to make sense of the moral and ethical contradictions. The dynamics of sense-making include sensing and constructing meaning, the importance of affective responses and cultural context, and concerns and interests.[20] The long-term outcome of an organizational public moral failure which can result in dissolution or transformation and renewal will be determined by how the moral and ethical contradictions are understood.

In other research, Frederick Bird has identified the impact of cultural factors and individual causes on moral silence, moral deafness and moral blindness in organizations.[21] Cultural factors include beliefs, philosophy, role of legal action, beliefs regarding the inevitability of outcomes and an ethos of tolerance. Individual causes include fear of involvement and implication, resignation, futility, other preoccupations and ethical inarticulacy.

Institutionally, there is also a cost to maintaining silence: this translates into loss of organizational focus, time and energy to achieve the good, and a corrosion of the moral and ethical life of the organization. The implications of organizational silence on decision making and the change process are profound. Lack of a variety of input and of critical analysis of ideas and alternatives leads to less efficient organizational decision making; lack of negative internal feedback resulting in poor detection of error and limited self-improvement; and ineffective organizational change. Silence creates dissatisfaction, stress and cynicism in an organization. The effects of organizational silence on employees can be devastating. The experience of having no voice can result in employee non-involvement, sabotage and even withdrawal from the organization.[22]

Church-specific factors fostering silence and denial

"... nothing is covered up that will not be uncovered, and nothing secret that will not become known." (Matthew 10:26-28)

Insights from organizational studies can help reveal Church-specific factors that have fostered silence and denial in the ongoing clergy sexual abuse crisis. Despite the rhetoric of virtue, character and conscience, the Church tends to promote moral responsibility by obedience to rules and laws.[23] In chapter 2, we explored the role of a sin-centred, act-oriented moral theology and the primacy of obedience to Church authority for their effect on moral sensitivity to harms done. The Church's internal canon law, which has been privileged over civil law, has clearly created a sense of special and highly secret consideration for the sins of clergy.[24] Exhortations from the pulpit and from magisterial documents related to ethical sensitivity to wrongdoing and the courage to speak truth to power have been directed outward to the sins of the world, not the sins of the Church.

Also, a certain theological understanding of the Church as the perfect society has rendered many incapable of discussing ecclesial sin.[25] While the Catholic Church is focused on rules and laws in general, it has no code of professional ethics for its clergy. While ordination legitimates professional authority and confers the power to execute priestly functions – that is, to access the sacred – it does not extend to all administrative activity.[26]

The culture of the Church is hierarchical, patriarchal, monarchical and clerical. All in formal Church leadership in the Roman Catholic Church are male and celibate. They have all been prepared for priesthood in a closed seminary formation where obedience and loyalty are privileged virtues, and dissent and disagreement are bad.[27] The theology of the priesthood understands the ordained as ontologically or essentially different from the non-ordained. The holiness of the state of priesthood becomes equated with the holiness of individual priests. The ordained priesthood overshadows the priesthood of the baptized. In chapter 3 we reviewed the distinction between clergy and laity and saw that celibacy has served to present clergy as holier than ordinary mortals.

The institutional Church demonstrates high vertical differentiation between ordained and laity. The educational background of bishops is slightly varied, but is dominated by men who have been seminary and university professors, with a high predominance of moral theology and canon law backgrounds. Moreover, Church leadership is understood as divinely appointed, with direct descent from the original apostles. There is hierarchy even within the ranks of the ordained: deacons, priests, monsignors, bishops, and then the honorific Cardinals.

Clericalism – which has been defined as "the conscious or unconscious concern to protect the particular interests of the clergy and to protect the privilege and power that traditionally has been conceded to those in the clerical state" – promoted denial and secrecy.[28] Church culture is highly dominated by promises of fidelity, the "pontifical secret" and oaths of obedience.[29] At the 2019 Summit, Cardinal Marx said objections to transparency

> are mainly directed against violations of pontifical secrecy, as well as ruining the reputation of innocent priests or of the priesthood and the Church as a whole through false accusations, if these are spread … Every objection based on pontifical secrecy would only be relevant if compelling reasons could be shown why pontifical secrecy should apply to the prosecution of criminal offences concerning the abuse of minors. As things stand, I know of no such reasons.

The organizational culture of the Church prohibits transparency. It fosters only the narrowest and most vertical accountability: priest to bishop; bishop to Rome; and none to the laity. There is basically one-way communication in the Church from the top down, manifesting a clear distinction between the teaching Church and the learning Church.[30] There is high control over information. There are serious powers of silencing, and even excommunication from the Church.[31] Whistleblowers are marginalized.[32]

Reporting of sexual offences was discouraged. Inappropriate use of professional secrecy and even of the secrecy of the confessional – victims were told that *their* talking about their abuser was a violation of the secrecy of the confessional – occurred often. Also, the powerful secrecy surrounding sexuality made this a particularly difficult topic for any conversation. All these features provide the elements for a perfect storm of silence and denial in the Church.

A new commitment to dialogue

> *But speaking the truth in love, we must grow up in every way into him who is the head, into Christ, from whom the whole body, joined and knit together by every ligament with which it is equipped, as each part is working properly, promotes the body's growth in building itself up in love. (Ephesians 4:15-16)*

Often there has been active resistance to lay-led initiatives. These include victim-survivor groups that do the important work of making sense of the crisis. Sometimes discussion groups are forbidden to use Church property. Breaking the silence and denial that dominated the clergy sexual abuse crisis is critically important. It calls for a new era of open and courageous communication in the Church and about the Church. The Second Vatican Council replaced a style of decision making and communication that was in direct response to the Protestant Reformation and the First Vatican Council (1869–1870), which emphasized one-way communication from Rome, to bishops, to clergy, to laity. On the doctrinal level, it articulated the communicative nature of God's revelation, the liturgy, the nature and mission of the Church, and the Church's relation to the world. It also presented a range of dialogical practices for a range of Church activity when it spoke of *collegiality* among bishops, *collaboration* with laity, *consultation* with theologians and *dialogue* with the world.

We communicate beliefs, values, hopes and fears in many ways. Some involve speech and language, but we also communicate through our symbols, rituals, sacraments, music, art, poetry and stories. Conversations are generally personal and intimate. Dialogue refers to a dynamic communication, with all participants functioning as both speakers and listeners. As Hinze has elegantly demonstrated, in the Church this takes the public forms of hearings, plenary sessions at synods and episcopal conferences, but also happens in liturgy, homilies and adult catechesis.[33] However, the strange dialogue of the old Baltimore catechism, where answers were provided for the learner even before the question was meaningful, has taught many Catholics a twisted sense of dialogue.

After generations of passive participation, *Lumen Gentium*, Vatican II's Dogmatic Constitution on the Church, recognized that the laity are, "by reason of the knowledge, competence or outstanding ability which they may enjoy, permitted and sometimes even obliged to express their opinion on those things which concern the good of

85

the Church."[34] Dialogue is key to fostering an understanding of both individual and ecclesial limitations and sinfulness.

There are real challenges for meaningful dialogue in the computer age of blogs and social media. Meaningful dialogue between disciples of Christ requires recognition and respect for the gifts of all in the Church. This dialogue is much more than politically correct democratic discussion run by Robert's Rules of Order. This dialogue involves both active listening and courageous speech. An ethic for precisely this kind of dialogue was described in Cardinal Joseph Bernardin's *Catholic Common Ground Initiative: Foundational Documents*. This publication outlined an ethic and a path for dialogue in and about the Church, including these points:

> - no single group or viewpoint in the Church has a monopoly on the truth.
> - no one or group should judge itself to be 'the saving remnant'.
> - presume those with whom we differ are acting in good faith and detect insights and concerns.
> - avoid labels such as "the hierarchy", "radical feminists" and "conservatives" and "liberals".
> - bring the church to engage contemporary culture, acknowledging our culture's achievements and dangers.[35]

Theologically, there have been two approaches to dialogue. Bradford Hinze notes that "the first approach defines dialogue in terms of obedience, whereas the second defines obedience in terms of dialogue."[36] Understanding dialogue as imitating Jesus' obedience to the Father has its strengths. But it can limit dialogue to obedience to authority and a one-way approach to communication: from the top down. A dialogic approach that finds its inspiration in the life of the Trinity – where there is continual dynamic communication of love between Father, Son and Holy Spirit – brings demands for conversion that arise from the dialogue itself. This approach helps us to acknowledge the communal element in our life of faith and the mutually interdependent nature of faith and the sacraments.

Pastoral pause and prayer

> ➤ Can you recognize conspiracies of silence in your own family or work life?
> ➤ Have you ever felt silenced in a Church situation?
> ➤ What would you need to empower you to feel more confident in speaking up and speaking out in the face of wrongdoing? What would be the biggest obstacle to speaking up or out?
> ➤ What parish or diocesan action would begin a new commitment to meaningful dialogue in the Church?

Chapter 5

Reformation and Renewal for a Sick Soul

"I have come to call not the righteous but sinners to repentance." (Luke 5:32)

Introduction

Jesus entered into human history for our salvation. He came to restore our relationship with the Father through the power of the Holy Spirit: "If anyone is in Christ, there is a new creation: everything old has passed away; see, everything has become new!" (2 Corinthians 5:17-19). This new creation requires continual conversion to the mind of Christ.

In the first four chapters of this book, the history of clergy sexual abuse has revealed a deeply wounded and fractured Church. Church leadership response and insights from studies on the dynamics of this abuse manifest endemic – deep seated and multi-generational – ecclesial pathologies in need of deep spiritual and ecclesial reform and renewal if healing and long-term prevention are to occur. The history demonstrates that such reform will not come easily. There is both ongoing denial of the depth of the ecclesial pathology and of the polarizing diagnoses of the underlying pathology. I understand theology in the classic sense of St. Irenaeus's "faith seeking understanding." This is surely a time for persons of faith to receive help from formal theological analysis in understanding the challenges of reform demanded by the clergy sexual abuse crisis. I therefore wrote to David Deane, associate professor of theology at the Atlantic School of Theology in Halifax, Nova Scotia, for his assistance.

Dear Professor Deane,

I need your theological expertise for help in understanding the role of ongoing personal and ecclesial conversion and reform in the Church. I know there have been many reform movements in history. Can you provide me with an example of true reform that might serve as a model in responding to the clergy sexual abuse crisis? Can you offer me some insights into the theological roots of resistance to meaningful conversion and reformation? Finally, and important to me as a child of Vatican II, can you analyze why the reforms of the Second Vatican Council have failed to fulfill their promise?

Dear Sister Nuala,

Thank you for consulting me. I will respond to your questions in four sections.

> *I begin with an account of ongoing personal and ecclesial conversion and reform as absolutes in the Christian life.*
> *I then illustrate a period of effective reform, with implications for a response to the clergy abuse crisis, exploring the work of St. Peter Damian.*
> *Then I show that this reformation has been transformed since the Protestant Reformation, from an ontological imperative to a traumatic and divisive event. I also reflect on the failure of Vatican II reforms and lessons for us today.*
> *Finally, I share some of my hopes for the future of the Church.*

Ongoing personal and ecclesial conversion and reform as absolutes in the Christian life

In chapter 2, on the harms caused by the clergy sexual abuse of minors, we saw the righteous anger of the gentle Jesus when children are abused, harmed and disrespected. There are other times in the gospels when Jesus comes on very strong. Not with the poor, the sick, the vulnerable or sinners, such as tax collectors and prostitutes. To them he offers change and hope, a new world, forgiveness from sins and transformation. Jesus comes on strong when dealing with authority figures who don't know they need to repent and reform. "Woe to you, scribes and Pharisees, hypocrites!" Jesus says (Matthew 23:13). He calls them "snakes," "a brood of vipers," and asks them, terrifyingly, "How can you escape being sentenced to hell?" (Matthew 23:33). Throughout the gospels, two kinds of people approach Jesus: those who want to change (through healing or forgiveness) and those who either don't know they need to reform, or won't. The needy, the marginalized and sinners are in the first category. The pharisees, the scribes and the rich young man are in the second. The rich young man is better than most of us. He has kept the commandments since his youth. But when Jesus asks him to change, when Jesus calls him to genuine reform, "he was shocked and went away grieving" (Mark 10:17-22).

While we correctly emphasize the loving qualities Jesus displayed, the gospels are clear that Jesus, building on the ministry of John the Baptist, is calling people to radical reform. This the centrepiece of Jesus preaching, "Repent, for the kingdom of heaven has come near" (Matthew 3:2). Reform, repentance and conversion are at the core of Jesus' ministry; the gospels leave no room to doubt this. And from the beginning, many in power were very slow to accept the fact that following Jesus meant conversion and reform.

I will show how this understanding of reform, intrinsic to Jesus' ministry, has been understood in the Church's history. This is important because of the *form* reformation takes in such figures as Paul and the Church fathers. How can Paul be a reformer? The Church was new, so what was there to reform? The answer to this question underscores that this is not a reformation of a past embodiment of the Church, remembered nostalgically as a golden age: it is a reformation of Christ's body, which is the Church, past, present and future. We can reform a body by weight loss, exercise and even cosmetic surgery. A body is material: it has arms, legs and a head. The language of "body" is a metaphor. Its use here is compatible with the organic notion of Church and health metaphors used in this book. But the Body of Christ is also far more than metaphor.

To understand this, we need to move beyond the kind of mind / body or matter / spirit dualisms we often are trapped in. What happens at the Mass resists this kind of dualistic thinking and illustrates the way we need to be thinking if we are to grasp how Paul and the Church Fathers understood the reformation of Christ's body. They thought about bodies as "porous" to the Holy Spirit. This porousness enables the presence of the Spirit, who "Christifies" us: that is, the Spirit unites us with Christ.

When we think about reform as an imperative for the Church, we tend to think about structural and/or doctrinal reform. This way of thinking is not wrong. It imagines reform in terms of the two aspects of reality we can most easily imagine – the material or structural world – and the non-material world of thought and ideas. Again, this is not wrong. It is probable that we need to change structures in the Church and maybe change doctrines, too. But reform as a core element of the Christian life from day 1 was emphasized by Christians who did not see reality in terms of a dualism between material things and thought or spiritual things. If we are to understand reform in the history of the Church, we need to be aware of this. Further, the kind of reform that I think is necessary is beyond either material (structural) reform or doctrinal (thinking/believing) reform. It involves a reform of *what we are*. This reform can and will lead to structural and/or doctrinal reform, but such reforms flow from the core reform of what we are.

This is a complicated idea to grasp for us modern people who think in terms of binaries such as body/spirit and matter/thought. We don't have categories to draw on concepts that many earlier Christians did. Because of this, we often misread Paul's letter to the Romans, for example. In Romans 7 and 8, Paul talks about life according to the Spirit or life according to the flesh. These are the two modes of being in the world, with one bringing a world of peace and love, and one bringing sin and suffering. In the last 500 years, many people have assumed that when Paul talks about "according to the flesh" in Romans, he means that the body is bad. For Paul, though, the same body can be fuelled with the Spirit of God or driven only by its own base needs. The one body, which looks the same, can be different on an invisible level, as the Holy Spirit that animates it can never be seen. Paul is not a dualist. He believes that we can reform the Body of Christ in our bodies by acting in ways that accept the Holy Spirit into our "mortal bodies" (Romans 8:11). This is the heart of reform, a reformation of Christ in the bodies of women and men through the indwelling of the Holy Spirit in them.

For Paul in Romans, no law, no structure, no system can save us. We can't reform the structure and expect to be fine. No matter what the structure is, if the people in it are not fuelled by the Spirit, they cannot do what is good, as the Spirit is the good. Neither can doctrine save us. For Paul, we can profess the law of Moses, but without transformation of who we are, we will just compete with one another to be the most holy or pious. And so the competition and pride that are at the heart of suffering in the world will continue. Thus, structural or doctrinal reform is not what is needed for Paul. Rather, it is the reform of the body of Jesus Christ in the bodies of women and men that is at the core of the Christian life. Structures and doctrines can flow from such people, but structures and doctrines can't reform people.

So, too, the *Catechism of the Catholic Church* stresses that the Church is Marian before it is Petrine (no. 773). This is because at the annunciation, the Blessed Mother accepts the Holy Spirit, leading to the presence of Christ within her. This is the form of the Church – a "yes" to the Holy Spirit, who leads to the presence of Christ within. With the Blessed Mother, this presence of Christ formed in her womb is material and substantial. For us, Christ, whom we accept through the Holy Spirit, is reformed substantially but not materially. But in both, where Christ is, there the Church is. Christ is present in the material world in the bodies of men and women. Christ acts and works through and with them.

Christ calls us to do things that are not easy for us by nature. He does not retaliate with violence to defend himself but risks all, loves all and follows God's will to the point of suffering and death. This is not natural, but it is possible, because in embodied acts like prayer, peacefulness and charity, we are saying "yes" to the Holy Spirit. This "yes" leads to union between us and the Holy Spirit: "If the Spirit of him who raised Jesus from the dead dwells in you, he who raised Christ from the dead will give life to your mortal bodies also through his Spirit that dwells in you" (Romans 8:11). The indwelling of the Spirit is not a metaphor. It happens here and now, in our "mortal bodies." The Holy Spirit, who is one with the Son, leads to the real and substantial presence of the Son in us. This is not a material presence, as in Mary's womb, or simply a metaphorical or symbolic presence. The Holy Spirit, accepted into our bodies, unifies us with Christ who comes to dwell within us. Paul emphasizes this when he writes, "it is no longer I who live, but it is Christ who lives in me" (Galatians 2:20). Thus, persons can become Christ-like through an embodied acceptance of the Holy Spirit. This enables them to reform Christ's body by being transformed into a part of the Body of Christ.

When we repent and accept Jesus' radical call, it is to something wholly different. In embodied action, we accept this call through the work of the Holy Spirit, who unites us with Christ and makes possible radical action. Such radical action includes faith, hope, love, sacrifice for the poor, giving up the wisdom of profit and self-assertion, and humbling ourselves. It involves seeing the victims of sexual abuse as one with the broken, abused and crucified Christ, and serving their needs rather than working to preserve the good name of an institution and avoiding scandal. Such self-preservation is normal human behaviour; only reformation to the mind of Christ can help loosen its hold on us. In the early Church, this is the understanding of reform. It is a core facet of what it means to be a Christian.

As time passes, this personal reformation, called for by Christ, quickly becomes seen as communal when the Church looks at ways that it can better participate in Christ's mission. This is evident after Constantine's decriminalization of Christianity with the Edict of Milan in 313. By then, Christians comprised half the population of Rome, and the Church could look at itself, its teaching and practices, and work for structural reform. From the fourth century on, the Church adopts a more catholic (in the sense of universal) approach to reform. The focus on Church structures that becomes possible after Constantine is theologically consistent with the personal reforming of Christ's body that preceded it.

For example, Augustine sought to reform the episcopacy, critiquing bishops who seek eminence. He writes that the episcopate "is the name of a task, not an honor" and "hence a 'bishop' who has his heart set on a position of eminence rather than the opportunity for service should realize that he is no bishop" (*City of God*, 19:19). Augustine uses the word "bishop" twice. The episcopacy is a reality that can't be reduced to a word, title or office. Either the bishop is one with the servant Christ and is therefore a true bishop, or he is just a man with the crown and robe trappings of monarchy. The Christian is one in whom Christ dwells through the presence of the Holy Spirit; the bishop is a particular form of Christian based on a particular kind of indwelling. This indwelling comes from humility, servitude, courage and other embodied acts that are recognized by the Church. The title "bishop" does not make a true bishop. Augustine's calls for reform are ecclesial, but flow from the understanding of conversion and reformation that we see in the early Church.

The Church is the communal reality of conversion to, and reformation of, Christ's body. Thus ecclesial reform will, if it is faithful to Christ's call, mirror the conversion wherein the person comes to participate in Christ through the Holy Spirit. The Holy Spirit is the agent that enables the reformation of Christ's body. The Spirit's indwelling in the body of the person establishes the presence of Christ in her. But each person is substantially (in the non-material sense) united to others in whom the Spirit abides. In indwelling within the person, the Spirit establishes the substantial union of the person with Christ. If this is true, then the Spirit who indwells in bodies of women and men establishes these women and men as substantially one with each other. That substantial union is what we call the Church. It is not a building or a set of roles or offices: it is a substantial reality – the Holy Spirit in the bodies of women and men conforming them to Christ, whose body they re-form. Paul writes, "For as in one body we have many members, and not all the members have the same function, so we, who are many, are one body in Christ, and individually we are members one of another" (Romans 12:4). The Holy Spirit is not, for Paul, sealed up in individuals, with the Spirit's substantial integrity subordinate to ours. Rather, our substantial integrity is subordinate to God's. As God is one, then we who abide in God through the indwelling of the Spirit are part of a whole. As Paul says, "Now you are the body of Christ and individually members of it" (1 Corinthians 12:27).

Reformation is understood in the early Church as a call for the conversion of organization, structures and offices as the collective expression of personal conversion. We think of reform in terms of organizational renewal, the purging of undesirables, schism and the establishment of a new, "clean" organization. In thinking of it this way, we miss the very thing that makes Christian reform Christian: the ongoing reformation of the Body of Christ. This work requires acts, including penitential acts, that accept the Holy Spirit. Reformation in the first millennium is both personal and ecclesial.

An example of true reform in the history of the Church needed today

Acknowledging personal and ecclesial conversion and ongoing reformation to the Body of Christ as Christian absolutes is essential; otherwise, we disassociate reforms from the scripture and Tradition on which they are based. The Gregorian Reforms of the 11th and 12th centuries changed Church policy and structures; they seem much more in keeping with "reform" as we imagine it today. But their foundation is in discipleship.

Peter Damian was an extreme voice. He claimed that too many in the Church were pursuing temporal power and pleasures rather than remaining faithful to the radical witness of Christ. He left what he called the "opulence" of Benedictine Cluniac monasteries to pursue more rigorous spiritual practices in his hermitage. From there he wrote to popes and princes on the subject of reform. Damian's *Book of Gomorrah*,[1] addressed to Pope Leo IX, is of special interest because it almost eerily echoes aspects of today's sexual abuse crisis, according to what we have seen in the first three chapters of this book. He begins by outlining transgressions – specifically, sexual impropriety among clerics – and proceeds to speak about the structural layers that complicate the problem. He details how the issue is made more complex when the seal of the confessional is used to develop a culture of silence and how canon law has affected the problem. He argues that the Church should never use a logic of "need" to justify maintaining perpetrators in ecclesial service. He argues that "excessive" piety is insufficient to address the problem, and that deep spiritual conversion is necessary. In doing so, his work echoes our crisis today.

Peter seeks papal legislation to produce revised canons that can respond to the new crisis. His logic is that while the new law of Christ means that sins that warranted death in the Old Testament no longer result in such punishment, such sins are incompatible with the kind of reformation necessary for a life in the ecclesial ranks. He writes,

"Surely it is clear that a person who has been degraded by a crime deserving death is not reformed so as to receive an order of ecclesiastical rank by any sort of subsequent religious life." Thus, the perpetrator needs to be removed from ecclesial functioning. He asked Pope Leo to establish canons that defrock clerical perpetrators. Peter does not see them as being beyond redemption, but he does see them as being beyond the clerical state.

He also focuses on the systemic contexts in which the immoral acts and their cover-ups occur. This is what we would call the "power relationships" between higher-ranking clergy and lower-ranking clergy, between clergy and laity, between the providers of sacraments (such as confession and baptism) and those who receive such sacraments from the very person who "groomed" them in sin. He recognized that such structural embeddedness required a massive investigation and the overhaul of structures that enabled the transgressions and kept the perpetrators in ecclesial service. He appealed to Pope Leo:

> Consequently, we ask and humbly implore Your Clemency, if it is legitimate to speak, that you prudently inspect the decrees of the sacred canons which, nevertheless, are well known to you … You should approve spiritual and prudent men to consult about this necessary investigation and you should reply to us regarding these chapters so as to remove all scrupulous doubt from our breast.

While spiritual reform is at the centre of the Christian life, an investigation needs to be conducted and done transparently. The ascetic hermit St. Peter Damian was asking for significant, legislated reform in the face of a complex problem. Systemic pathologies required the kind of top-down legislation that was in contrast to the kinds of personal spiritual practices for which Peter was renowned.

To speak of Peter Damian as a whistleblower may appear anachronistic, but he knew he was risking becoming an outcast in the Church by calling these practices and cover-ups into question. Such radical action was necessary, he holds, for a reason known all too well by modern Catholics: "just as [those who denounced heretics] strove to bring the erring and those who were leaving back to the fold, so it is also our intention to prevent in whatever way possible those who are inside from leaving." To stop "those who are inside from leaving," Peter called for reform – and radical reform, at that. Leo's response is all too familiar. At first, he approved Peter's text, but was soon persuaded by the growing ecclesial consensus that Peter was going too far. Instead of following Peter's demands that offenders be immediately expelled, he decided to dismiss only those who were guilty of repeated offences. Despite this, Peter Damian's calls had a significant influence on his confrere Hildebrand, who became Pope Gregory VII. Gregory incorporated Peter's calls in a set of broader reforms on clerical celibacy that established the very legislation Peter was asking for.

Understanding resistance to conversion and reform

The Church today is in crisis. It desperately needs the conversion and reform we have just seen throughout its history. Thus, while the Church needs to reform, it is uniquely equipped to do so. Right? Sadly, wrong. In this section I respond to the question of why the Church resists reform and has grown almost incapable of it. This sounds depressing. And in part, it is. But if there are historical and cultural reasons for the Church's inability to reform in the modern world, these are not intrinsic to the body.[2] They are necroses – wounds resulting from trauma. As such, the diagnosis of these reasons gives cause for hope for healing and new life.

I'll share a personal analogy. Last year I was diagnosed with a liposarcoma, a dangerous and life-threatening form of cancer. When the tumour was removed, they found that it was a non-cancerous tumor that mimicked a liposarcoma because of trauma to the area. At one stage it seemed as if I would die from a fatal illness. However, the problem was caused by a necrosis: the death of cells resulting from past trauma to the area. Once it was repaired, I was returned to health. The Church's inability or unwillingness to reform is based on specific, identifiable traumas over the past 500 years. These traumas can be diagnosed; we might have a chance of treating the things they have led to. While there are a number of traumas that have impeded reform in the Church, I would like to focus on three: the Protestant Reformation, the rise of the nation-state, and modernity and polarizing divisions within the Church.

The first trauma is the Protestant Reformation. When we think about the word "reformation," what comes to mind is not the re-formation of Christ's body, which is at the core of the Christian life. What comes to mind is the Lutheran Reformation, the great schism in Western Christianity, which led to what amounts to some 47,000 distinct Christian denominations today. So, "reformation" is associated with past traumas and is a dirty word for Catholics. The primary Catholic response of the Counter-Reformation involved reforms that were seen as final. The Council of Trent (1545–1563) was understood as the definitive response to the Reformation, reforming the Church and strengthening it for the long struggle against Protestantism. It, along with Jesuit order and structure, established the Catholic Church as a well-organized, almost military machine that could endure the challenges of the modern world. In doing so, it emphasized military values of obedience, uniformity and strength. From this perspective, any calls for reform were understood in light of the schism that the Reformation represented. They were seen not as an act of Christian faith, but as a flouting of the obedience needed for the struggle with Protestantism. The flow of reforming zeal, intrinsic to the Christian life, stopped, and the Church began to calcify and grow fibrous.

A second trauma was the rise of the nation-state and the Church as a "perfect society." The Peace of Westphalia, which ended the post-Reformation wars, established the nation-state as the primary form of social order. This represented the ending of the Holy Roman Empire and the shift in power not simply from Church to state, but from divine power to secular: that is, *material* power. Today we think of power in largely modern, secular ways. For example, many speak about the changes in the Church associated with Constantine as a "compromise," with Christians "selling out" to attain political power. But ancients could not imagine subordinating divine power to political power. Power and "the real" was understood to be the divine. The immaterial divine was far more significant than material things.

In the modern world, "the real" is material. The nation-state, coming into being at the same time, is the political and organizational expression of this principle. As we saw earlier, when we think of "substance," we think of something material. Pre-modern people didn't. For them, material things decompose, corrupt and die. Material things' grasp of reality is fleeting. Therefore, they couldn't be seen as real and unchangeable. Power was once understood to be God. Things in the world, which could participate in God, could participate in this power. At least from the 17th century on, power comes to lie in social orders that are established not in divine will, but in the will of the people in votes or uprisings of the populace.

The Church was threatened massively. Conceptually, it was an anachronism, in that it was based on an understanding of the real that involved the material and immaterial, time and eternity, heaven and earth and their relations. In contrast, in the modern world "the real" was being reduced to things visible, measurable and quantifiable. All else was given the status of opinion or fancy, including faith in God. It has become common to speak about "the age of faith" giving way to "the age of reason." In reality, it was the dawn of an age with an abridged model of reason, reduced to things measurable sand quantifiable. It was the dawn of an era that ruptured the world in which the Church grew and prospered, and the world with which the Church, 300 years later, is still struggling to come to terms. Also, the political expressions of this world literally threatened the Church. Napoleon held the Pope under house arrest. He was later threatened by emerging Italian nationalism under Garibaldi. In a world of nation-states with rulers and armies, the Church and the papacy were increasingly isolated and helpless.

The Church responded to this crisis in a way that has made reform almost unimaginable in the modern world. First, the Church sought not to contest but to mirror the developing nation-state and the model of reason on which it was based. Through a series of treaties, over time, the Vatican itself became a nation-state. Leo XIII's 1885 Encyclical *Immortale Dei* (On the Christian Constitution of States) is one of many attempts to navigate this new world, in which the Church is surrounded by nation-states whose foundational ideology is antithetical to her own. In it, Leo asserts the Church's superiority over these societies, but through seeing the Church itself as a society echoing modern forms. As he writes, "For the only-begotten Son of God established on earth a society which is called the Church … it is to be understood that the Church … is a society perfect in its own nature and its own right."[3]

The modern world brought a crisis to the Church.[4] The response to this crisis was to increasingly imagine the Church in ways that owed more to modern philosophy than to the theology we discussed when we looked at Paul and the annunciation earlier in this chapter. The Church itself becomes seen, rather than a group of women and men, flawed and fallen, capable of hope and love and charity through participating in God, who alone is perfect. No, in this world the Church comes to understand itself as a *societas perfecta*, perfect in its material and societal expression. In the pre-modern world, perfection could only be part of the non-material world. In the modern world, with such concepts losing their hold, perfection was increasingly seen in the Church's own material reality. This is an impediment to reform because reform involves an understanding of the good (Christ) and a body that needs to reform to be more Christ-like. But when the body itself is understood as perfect, or even wholly good in itself, then there is nothing *to* reform. Further, and even more damagingly, if the Church is *societas perfecta*, then any critique must, necessarily, be evil. Therefore, reformation is not only impossible (the Church being a perfect society), it is also an evil impulse in that it seeks to alter, change and thereby detract from "perfection." This notion of *societas perfecta* does not merely make reform impossible (how do you reform perfection?), but also it fuels the sexual abuse crisis in more direct ways. If responding to the needs of a victim of sexual abuse means tarnishing the good name of the Church, or damaging the Church itself, then responding to the victim's needs is an immoral act, as it damages or tarnishes the good. The concept of *societas perfecta* therefore both renders reform impossible and encourages what we would see as evil acts – acts that seek to preserve the good name of the Church by covering up the abuse of minors.

A third trauma is the modern polarization of "liberal" and "conservative" worldviews and agendas. In chapter 3, we saw the corrosive power of these divisions today. Historically, people did not understand themselves – or political or ecclesial processes – in terms of these categories. This came into being through the grand narrative modernity tells itself. It leads to one side seeing the past as technologically and intellectually limited, and therefore "progress" from this past as positive. This narrative is embedded in the modern world. When we see atrocities being committed, we call them "medieval"; we refer to the past as "the dark ages." In contrast, a perspective emerges very soon after the French Revolution in the late 18th century, seeing the forces unleashed in the "brave new world" as dangerous and threatening. Some variants of this narrative see the past not as dark and ignorant, but as golden and idyllic. The goal is not to *progress* further away from this idealized past, but somehow to return to it.

In the modern world, we define ourselves as liberal or conservative. We pick sides, and friends, based on these tribal identifications. There is no reason why the Catholic Church, a body that predates the modern world, should be subject to its categories. But it is. Media outlets choose sides and offer a consistent ideological agenda. Some people read *First Things*, and some read the *National Catholic Reporter*.

When Pope Francis speaks, people ask, "Is this on our side or the other side? Is this a broadside against liberals or a rebuke of conservatives?" The secular media, schooled in this core Left vs Right narrative of the modern age, can report it no other way than through the grand metanarrative of our age. These stories – of progress and liberation, or insanity and destruction – are the categories through which we understand our world.

Sometimes we can be so trapped within our worldview that we interpret everything else in light of it. Because of this, every move, every attempt at renewal or reform, is processed through the lenses of liberalism and conservativism. A papal pronouncement is quickly scanned: Does it mention abortion? If so, maybe it can be applauded by conservatives. Does it use the word "inclusive" or "diverse"? If so, it can be applauded by liberals. So how can Catholicism reform when there are no actual Catholics to do the reforming? If there are only liberals and conservatives who subordinate Catholicism to their own political and ecclesial ideology, then any meaningful attempts at reform will further divide the Church and risk true schism. The Church has always had divisions, but today's polarization is qualitatively different. Like the other traumas discussed, polarization impedes reformation. Polarization permits no narrative to escape it; all narratives – even, horrifically, the sexual abuse crisis – become subordinate to it and serve as pawns in its own ideological game.

Lessons from the failure of the reforms of the Second Vatican Council

The Church has been struggling with the modern world for a long time. For much of the 19th century, the Church's response was a siege mentality. Part of this was justified. The modern world brings with it many things that should be resisted. But this siege mentality brought with it calcification and necrosis. The theology we looked at in the first section of this consultation was largely forgotten, codified in manuals that were recited by rote but never really understood. The

Church could not "talk back" to the modern world, but only recite phrases whose meaning had been long forgotten. In resisting the modern world, it had come to ape its worst features, with the Vatican becoming a nation-state, largely hostile to neighbours.

As the 20th century wore on, the realization that the Church was in need of reform grew. The Second Vatican Council represented the most significant attempt at ecclesial reform for centuries.[5] It is common to say that this was the most significant reform since Trent. (Reading the documents of Trent, one could argue that it was less open to true reform than the Second Vatican Council: a definitive response to the Protestant Reformation, rather than true reform, was Trent's driving principle.) The reforms of Vatican II sought to make the Church more participatory (*Lumen Gentium*), more connected to scripture (*Dei Verbum*), more ecumenical (*Unitatis Redintegratio*), more shaped by the laity (*Apostolicam Actuositatem*) and less insular (*Gaudium et Spes*). Overall, it aimed at nothing less than a New Pentecost, reforming the Church for the modern world. By the standards of Church history, it is too early to judge the impact of Vatican II. The necroses making the Church resistant to reform have impeded the goals of the Council from being realized. Here is one example. The final necrosis – polarization – has meant that the work of the Council was received by two distinct ecclesial cultures. These cultures both subordinated the Council to their own core narratives, effectively suffocating its voice.

Liberal Catholic culture has often favoured a nebulous "spirit" of the Council over the documents the council produced. Thus, an openness to positive elements within modern society became a subordination of Catholic theology to it. Some calls for the Church to be more democratic seem to establish modern social norms (which shape our worldview as modern Western subjects) as true. People with this aim seek to conform Catholic theology to these norms, whether or not there is sufficient basis in scripture or Tradition. One example is the exodus from clerical life in the West after the Council – an exodus that saw many swap life in the Church for life in service of the state (such as in social services). This move was based on the principle that the good can be better served by secular rather than religious life. This clerical exodus has been mirrored by an exodus of the laity – an exodus evident in parishes throughout the Western world. Since the Council, religious affiliation has been in freefall. More and more Catholics are constituted as late modern secular subjects rather than coherently Catholic ones. But there has also been a rise in the number of persons in the technologically developed nations who identify themselves as atheists or agnostics.

Conservative Catholic culture has often sought to undermine the Second Vatican Council. Moderate forms involve emphasizing a hermeneutic of continuity over a hermeneutic of rupture. Here the reforms are subject to "unbroken tradition"; Tradition becomes the Rosetta Stone interpreting Vatican II. As such, the reforms of the Council are rejected, while its coherence with older Church positions are affirmed. In more radical forms (which are increasingly visible in Catholic new media circles), the Second Vatican Council is seen as a moment of Babylonian captivity, where the Church was beholden to the spirit of the age. Thus, the Council should no more be taken as authoritative than are the pronouncements of a Pope who is being held captive under duress. In such quarters, the reforms are rejected from within with the kind of vehemence that schismatic bodies, like the Society of Saint Pius X, show from without.

Because of the necrosis caused by liberal and conservative polarization, the Church, since the Second Vatican Council, has been embroiled in an increasingly vicious battle over how to interpret the Council. Rather than seek to engage and unleash the reforms of the Council, some Catholics have seen its (temperate) affirmations of the modern world as an encouragement to move beyond Catholicism, either explicitly, through leaving, or implicitly, through being formal subjects of secular ideology rather than Catholic thought. Other Catholics have identified a (largely illusory) pre-modern Catholic empire as the good. They have sought to resist any conciliar reforms in favour of or seeking to rebuild this false (in the sense of historically inaccurate as well as ungodly) idol. The former side is on a "team" made up of the political left in whatever Western state they reside in, and the latter side is on a "team" of the political right in whatever Western state they reside in. These "teams," not Catholicism itself, shape their identity. Neither side has engaged the reforms, and still, over half a century later, we fight over how to interpret the Council rather than work to implement its reforms.

Hopes for personal conversion and ecclesial reform

All this paints an unhopeful picture. Hopelessness would be, however, naïve on three fronts. First, it would assume that the difficulties of the Church are unique. They are not. The world, St. Jerome said, "awoke with a groan to find itself Arian." This was *after* the Council of Nicaea (325), whose findings sought to overcome Arianism. The Council tried to establish theological principles, but they would take a hundred years to become engrained in the culture of the Church. Second, as the modern world wears on, we come to greater insights into the necrosis the Body of Christ has developed. For example, for decades we were too focused on the stereophonic nightmare of left vs right to be able to step back and diagnose our very participation in such polarization as a problem. Third, and more importantly, hopelessness would be naïve because the reform of the Church is primarily the activity of the Holy Spirit. The Holy Spirit has not given up on the Church.

Reform, as stressed at the outset, is at the core of the Christian life. It involves a "yes" to the Holy Spirit, a "yes" that leads to the presence of Christ within. This "yes" takes the form of embodied acts: acts of faith, hope and love. Such acts accept the union with Christ for which we are made. This personal conversion is the engine that drives communal and ecclesial conversion. We must (1) acknowledge that such conversion is needed, (2) be prepared to change, (3) diagnose the precise pathologies that need to be treated, and (4) commit to treating them effectively. This book is in the service of such an enterprise. The treatment requires an openness to Christ through the Holy Spirit – an openness that, due to fear and necrosis, we have struggled to find in the modern world. But the shock of the revelations of sexual abuse have, like a bellow from John the Baptist, made *metanoia* possible. *Metanoia* is a repentance that comes from the shock of having things revealed to us as they are. This revelation in turn makes possible the desire to accept Christ, substantially, in our bodies. This acceptance – personally, communally and ecclesially – is the form that reformation in the Church has taken in the past, and will be the form it takes again.

Dear Professor Deane,

Thank you for these insights on the essential nature of ongoing personal conversion and reform for followers of Christ. Your reflection helps in understanding much of the resistance to meaningful reform demonstrated in the history of the clergy abuse crisis. The role of belief about the Church as the "perfect society" is clearly a major factor. Polarizing views, not just legitimate differences from time, place and culture, are shown to be contrary to the fundamental unity of the Church.

Pastoral pause and prayer

> How open are you to deep spiritual conversion?
> How have you understood the Church as a "perfect society"?
> Are you being called to face biases and beliefs in Church teaching and practice contrary to "the mind of Christ"?
> Do you participate in polarizing and divisive judgments about 'others' in the Church?

Chapter 6

Healing Power and Relationships in the Church

"Learn from me; for I am gentle and humble in heart." (Matthew 11:29)

Introduction

Jesus was recognized as doing deeds of power throughout his ministry of healing and reconciliation. He was acutely aware that "power had gone forth from him" in his healing of the broken and marginalized woman with the hemorrhage (Mark 5:30). Indeed, we are disciples today through the good and transformative power of the Holy Spirit.

But Jesus himself had a profound experience as a victim of abuse of power throughout his Passion and death. This is dramatically demonstrated when he is taunted by Pilate, who said to him, "Do you refuse to speak to me? Do you not know that I have power to release you, and power to crucify you?" (John 19:10-11). Jesus does not respond with violence and retaliation, but reminds Pilate of the source of all power and allows himself to be crucified. He learned well from his mother, Mary. In her Magnificat, she exclaims that "He has brought down the powerful from their thrones, and lifted up the lowly: he has filled the hungry with good things, and sent the rich away empty" (Luke 1:52-53). She recognizes the limits of earthly power just as she is filled with the power of God. Jesus' teaching of the Beatitudes overturns conventions about power and earthly authority and ensures that he will be put to death. As Jesus said, "'Prophets are not without honour, except in their hometown, and among their own kin, and in their own house.' And he could do no deed of power there, except he laid hands on a few sick people and cured them. And he was amazed at their unbelief" (Mark 6:4-6).

In employing medical metaphors to clergy sexual abuse, we have seen not only the importance of a correct diagnosis but also its complexity. Crucially, a medical assessment needs to discover the essential nature of the illness and disease before it can be healed or cured. In reflecting on the abuse of power in the crisis, we need to ask if it is embedded in our genes. "Power tends to corrupt and absolute power corrupts absolutely,"[1] as Lord Acton once said. From our review of the history and dynamics of the clergy abuse crisis, we now need to investigate whether spiritual power inherently corrupts spiritually. Or is abuse of power so entrenched in our family history that it is accepted as normal functioning? How can and must the abuse be treated?

Sexual abuse of the vulnerable is primarily an abuse of power and position. This whole sexual crisis is deeply linked with power and the way power works in the Church at all levels. Every human institution revolves around the use of power. It is a complex phenomenon that can be used for service and healing or for domination and oppression. It is everywhere, both visible and hidden. By its nature, power is asymmetrical and depends highly on situation and social status. Power relationships in the Church require critically constructive analysis; in this chapter, we reflect on some key elements. Regrettably, and with tragic consequences, the Church has often been infected by this same culture of control.

We will identify the abuse of power and authority in all elements of the abuse crisis and reflect on it through Jesus' understanding of and witness to power. Then we will assess the culture of the Church in the clergy–laity distinction, clericalism and the exclusion of women from

109

formal leadership. Finally, we will explore new ways of empowering individual, community and leadership response.

The abuse of power and authority

In chapter 1, we heard Pope Francis identify the diseases of leadership in the Church, with particular attention to "a pathology of power and narcissism ... and the cancer of closed circles and careerism." In chapter 2, the abuse of power and authority was shown to be a significant element in the dynamics of the sexual abuse of minors in families, in society and in the Church. Abuse of power has been seen in the individual victimization and in leadership responses. With individual victims, even spiritual powers and authority were used in threats of damnation and expulsion from the Church for victims and their families. In what is surely a sin crying out for justice, clergy often used their authority and status as representing Christ himself to justify their abuse. Pope Francis, at the conclusion of the Summit, explicitly acknowledged that "It is difficult to grasp the phenomenon of the sexual abuse of minors without considering power, since it is always the result of an abuse of power, an exploitation of the inferiority and vulnerability of the abused, which makes possible the manipulation of their conscience and of their psychological and physical weakness."

Leadership responses that protected the Church's image and the institution and aimed to avoid scandal and conduct a frank cover-up of known offenders were clear abuses of authority. Legal manoeuvres such as using statutes of limitations – and opposing their reform in light of what is now known about the time lag between most offenses and their disclosure – to avoid moral responsibility and public accountability are reprehensible abuses of power and authority. Demands for gag orders and the maintenance of secrecy in settlements revictimized many. Many bishops and other Church leaders did not even enforce the canon law of the Church.[2]

The history demonstrates responses from Church leaders that transcend national and cultural differences that point to the culture of the Church itself. At the Summit, Cardinal Blase Cupich of Chicago recognized this as he said, "A process that merely changes policies, even if it is the fruit of the finest acts of collegiality, is not enough. It is the conversion of men and women throughout the entire Church – parents and priests, catechists and religious, parish leaders and bishops – and the conversion of ecclesial cultures on every continent that we must seek."

The history and dynamics of clergy sexual abuse highlight the special status of clergy and powerlessness of the laity in prevention and protection. Chapter 4's reflection on silence, denial and the avoidance of scandal emphasizes that structures and practices have colluded to create the experience of powerlessness for laity. This powerlessness is an emotional experience and a judgment about role, context and resources.

Jesus and power

Biblical stories graphically describe God's exercise of power and authority in the history of salvation.[3] God's power is always on the side of the poor, oppressed and vulnerable, to whom God manifests love and care. Jesus enters into human history as the ultimate manifestation of God's power and love. Overturning all conventions about seeking and holding on to power, Jesus empties himself for us and our salvation:

> though he was in the form of God, [he] did not regard equality with God as something to be exploited, but emptied himself, taking the form of a slave, being born in human likeness. And being found in human form, he humbled himself and became obedient to the point of death – even death on a cross. (Philippians 2:6-8)

Paradoxically, his emptying results in an abundance of power for Jesus. He uses power to heal and reconcile, never to dominate. It is power for and never over others. At the Last Supper, before he gives us the Eucharist, Jesus disconcerts his disciples.

[He] got up from table, took off his outer robe, and tied a
towel around himself. Then he poured water into a basin and
began to wash the disciples' feet and to wipe them with the
towel that was tied around him ... After he had washed their
feet, had put on his robe, and had returned to the table, he
said to them, "Do you know what I have done to you? You
call me Teacher and Lord – and you are right, for that is what
I am. So if I, your Lord and Teacher, have washed your feet,
you also ought to wash one another's feet. For I have set you
an example, that you also should do as I have done to you."
(John 13:4-5, 12-15)

Abuse of power in today's Church shows we are still trying to
figure out exactly what Jesus did in his example of servant leadership. Mysteriously, he did this just before he gave us the great gift of
Eucharist.

The frightened disciples who ran away and hid during the cruci-
fixion are transformed days later into courageous proclaimers of the
gospel through the power of the Holy Spirit. The Church was birthed
at Pentecost with the sending of the Spirit. We need to reclaim and
renew the power of the Holy Spirit and the doctrine of the Trinity
that we proclaim every time we bless ourselves and recite the Creed.
This is the Trinity of equality and mutual love, not the hierarchy we
have created of God the Father, then the Son and, last and often least,
the Holy Spirit. This equality and mutual love characterized the early
Church. The New Testament refers only to Jesus as "priest." It also
refers to the priesthood of all the baptized: "you are a chosen race, a
royal priesthood, a holy nation" (1 Peter 2:9-10).

The culture of the Church

There are now careful studies on the abuse of power in the Church in
general and in the clergy abuse crisis in particular from a variety of
perspectives, including Frawley-O'Dea,[4] Berry and Renner,[5] Higgins

and Letson,[6] and Robinson.[7] The culture of the Church is identified as a factor in all these studies. Irish bishops responding to the Murphy Report named the issue directly: "We are deeply shocked by the scale and depravity of the abuse as described in the Report. We are shamed by the extent to which child sexual abuse was covered up in the Archdiocese of Dublin and recognize that this indicates a culture that was widespread in the Church."[8]

In sharp contrast with early Christianity, the culture of the Church is imperial, hierarchical, monarchical, patriarchal and clerical.[9] How did such a radical shift occur? What do we even mean by "culture"? One description of culture is an essentially meaningful arrangement of society (*relationships*), ideology (*ways of thinking and valuing*) and technology (*means regarding material things*). Relationships, values and means reinforce each other. In particular, the arrangement of these three elements shapes the use of power and authority. It is extremely difficult to assess and critique a culture from within. Cultures, with their relationships and values, are crucial for human identity and contain positive and nourishing elements. But they also have a dark side: "a more concealed set of subjective attitudes often assimilated unconsciously over a long time. Together these habits of acting and interpreting can either imprison people within prejudices or they can become avenues toward authentic living, toward self-transcending choices that challenge the negative bias of any culture."[10] What are the prejudices and negative biases in Church culture that foster abuse of power?

Secular organizational research can help critique Church culture. Leaders are recognized as critical in creating the culture of an organization.[11] They have structural/hierarchical power related to authority and position and prestige power. The influence of power and self-focus in leaders can adversely affect their ability to respond to moral issues because they tend to be overconfident, fail to appreciate input from others, and misread situations as a result. [12]Addiction to power and denial are connected: leaders will use defense mechanisms such as hiding, ignoring or changing information to avoid embarrassing, threatening or painful situations.[13] In the Church, all leaders are ordained sacramentally and have enormous structural/hierarchical power, authority and tenure. They hold unique prestige power fostered by theologies of priesthood and an understanding of the ordained as being *in persona Christi* (in the person of Christ).

Catholic anthropologist Fr. Gerry Arbuckle defines bullying as

an act of violence involving the abuse of power by individuals, groups, institutions, or cultures, so that individuals or groups, not in a position to defend themselves are downgraded as human persons through being persistently subjected to threats of psychological, physical or cultural violence which weakens their self-confidence and self-esteem, so facilitating their subjugation.[14]

He identifies a number of cultures of bullying. The hierarchical and accountability-failure models are particularly relevant to abuse of power in the Church. How did the radical equality of the early Church become the hierarchical and patriarchal institution of today?

Let's review some relevant history on this shift found in *Healing the Church*.

How did the clergy–laity distinction become a characteristic of Catholicism?

Distinctions between clergy and laity were unheard of in the early Church. There, only Jesus is referred to as *priest*. The cultic sacrifices of priests in other religions were understood to have been completed in the ultimate sacrifice of the High Priest, Jesus. Early Christians met in familiar and intimate spaces of upstairs rooms and houses for reflection on ministry and for sharing of the Eucharistic meal. The primary elder or presbyter presided over the meal.

Ministry in the ancient church is all about action, not cultic worship. Outward-moving evangelization, preaching, teaching, and assembly leadership are the core ministries that constitute the Christian way of life. These actions, fundamentally the way a Christian lives his or her life, comprise the sacrifice, the liturgy, and the common priestly office of the whole people.[15]

The early Christian community is a *diakonia* or service community, gifted through baptism with charisms for the sake of the whole Church.

> Now there are varieties of gifts, but the same Spirit; and there are varieties of services, but the same Lord; and there are varieties of activities, but it is the same God who activates all of them in everyone. To each is given the manifestation of the Spirit for the common good. (1 Corinthians 12:4-7)

The gifts of all were valued and clearly understood to be needed by the Church.

By the end of the first century, individuals in the Christian community come to form the *clerus*, the Lord's portion or share, designating a group for spiritual and leadership functions in the growing community. The first use of laity, as distinct from clergy, appears in the First Letter from Clement at the end of the first century, and then not again until Clement of Alexandria uses it in the *Didascalia Apostolorum*. By the fourth and fifth centuries, the distinction becomes fixed. Constantine's Edict of Milan in 313 makes Christianity the state religion and there is a phenomenal increase in Church membership. The Eucharist moves from homes and intimate spaces into large imperial buildings, which become the basilica churches to accommodate the crowds. As with all large organizations, we see the development of a clergy and a hierarchy. Bishops become officials of the Roman Empire. *Ordinatio,* a Roman term for appointing to Roman civil office, is now used for the priests. As centuries pass, "We have here the beginning of a great reversal: symbols and legal positions dispensed grace rather than grace begetting life through charisms realized in office and service."[16]

By the time of the Council of Nicaea in 325, bishops have increasing power and presbyters shift from being advisors to the bishop to helpers in the celebration of Eucharist. Presiders over the Eucharist are increasingly understood in priestly/sacrificial terms. By the fifth century, priests are understood almost exclusively in their cultic role, and the Eucharist is celebrated in large basilicas that separate priests in the sanctuary from people in the pews. The Eucharist becomes more inward and focused on the presider as sacredness and mystery are emphasized. It is removed from the people as the priest is regarded as the only one holy enough to approach the "sacred mysteries." Proximity to the Eucharist comes to mean that ordination to priesthood conveys a permanent indelible character that changes the man's essence. The Council of Florence in 1439 first mentions an "ontological" change in the priest as a result of ordination. This exalted, essentially different character of the priest is captured in the 1566 *Catechism of the Council of Trent*:

> In the first place, then the faithful should be shown how great is the dignity and excellence of this sacrament considered in its highest degree, the priesthood. Bishops and priests being, as they are, God's interpreters and ambassadors, empowered in his name to teach mankind the divine law and rules of conduct and holding, as they do, His place on earth, it is evident that no nobler function than theirs can be imagined. Justly therefore are they called not only Angels but even gods, because of the fact that they exercise in our midst the power and prerogatives of the immortal God.

Bishops and priests as angels and even gods! This appears to be a remarkable contrast to the witness of Jesus himself.

> ... though he was in the form of God, [he] did not regard equality with God as something to be exploited, but emptied himself, taking the form of a slave, being born in human likeness. And being found in human form, he humbled himself,

and became obedient to the point of death – even death on a cross. (Philippians 2:6-8)

The requirement for mandatory celibacy in the Western Church emphasizes this angelic designation and understanding of the priest as one who is fundamentally different in nature to other human beings. From the Council of Elvira in 305, clergy were required to abstain from sex with their wives before assisting at the altar. Cultic purity had become crucial. Not surprisingly, then, "Celibacy, in this worldview, is the natural complement to the perfection of the ordained who are closest to the Eucharist and different in kind over the laity."[17]

The Lateran Council IV in 1215 mandates celibacy across the Western Church. There were also practical reasons for celibacy, related to the cleric's property and no progeny to inherit or heirs to contest hierarchical authority and power, but cultic purity figured strongly in the decision.

So, the first thousand years of the Church witnessed an inexorable separation of clergy and laity; the second thousand years have confirmed this separation.[18] We also saw the separation of the celebration of the Eucharist and ministry and the rejection of the theology of the gifts of all. The laity, the non-ordained, is reduced to the role of observers of the life of the Church.[19]

The fact that Pope Benedict opened the 2009–2010 Year for Priests, a year that saw escalating issues of clergy sexual abuse worldwide, with the quote "After God, the priest is everything!" demonstrates that the clericalization of the Church is alive and well. Throughout that year, priests went off together to study the meaning of priesthood, as if it could be understood without the participation of the laity. The sense of mutual interdependence is replaced by an exalted priestly status. Small wonder that priests and bishops considered themselves above the law in the case of clergy sexual abuse, and that laity defer to them as holier and of special status.

This is the culture in which we were formed and in which the clergy sexual abuse of minors has occurred. It has been inadequately dealt with for centuries. It is imperial, monarchical, hierarchical, patriarchal and clerical. How different it is from *Lumen Gentium*'s "For the distinction which the Lord made between sacred ministers and the rest of the People of God bears within it a certain union, since pastors and the other faithful are bound to each other by a mutual need" (no. 32)! In chapter 4 we reflected on the operative theologies of the Church, the episcopacy and the priesthood for their role. The theologies and associated canon law have been written by men who are clerics and deeply embedded in Church culture. Here we will briefly reflect on two specific elements requiring deeper consideration: clericalism and the role of women in the Church.

Clericalism

Everybody is talking about clericalism's role in the clergy sexual abuse crisis. In his 2018 Letter to the People of God, Pope Francis states clearly that clericalism is an approach that "not only nullifies the character of Christians, but also tends to diminish and undervalue the baptismal grace that the Holy Spirit has placed in the heart of our people."[20] Clericalism, whether fostered by priests themselves or by lay persons, leads to an excision in the ecclesial body that supports and helps to perpetuate many of the evils we condemn today. To say no to abuse is to say an emphatic no to all forms of clericalism. Clericalism is an important element in the diagnosis of clergy sexual abuse and the failure of Church leadership response.

Clericalism has been defined as

> the conscious or unconscious concern to protect the particular interests of the clergy and to protect the privilege and power that traditionally has been conceded to those in the clerical state. Among its chief manifestations are an authoritarian style of ministerial leadership, a rigidly hierarchical worldview, and a virtual identification of the holiness and grace of the church with the clerical state and thereby with the cleric himself.[21]

118

Clericalism protects the interests of the clergy and plays a major role in secrecy and non-accountability, as well as resistance to critique and reform.

Fr. George Wilson has provided a thoughtful analysis of the characteristics of clericalism:

- automatic status (by reason of position)
- power and authority conferred by position
- expertise assumed because of position
- embodiments of special status: dress, address and "perks" of lavish lifestyles
- protection of image (personal and institutional)
- resistance to critique
- resistance to change
- secrecy
- non-accountability.[22]

Each of these characteristics demonstrates and reinforces values, attitudes and practices. Each is worth consideration for its effects on ordained and lay alike. The notion of the common priesthood of all the baptized is corrupted. Finally, there is loss of touch with both the vocational call and with those whom they are called to serve. It is clear that "Clericalism … is always dysfunctional and haughty, crippling the spiritual and emotional maturity of the priest, bishop, or deacon caught in its web. Clericalism may command a superficial deference, but it blocks honest human communication and ultimately leaves the cleric practicing it isolated."[23] Clericalism is about attitude and perspective. It is not a new phenomenon; it has been manifested in very different political and social environments (culture). Insofar as it is elitist, it is sinful, in contradiction of the radical equality of the gospel and baptism. As Cardinal Cupich said at the 2019 Summit,

Perhaps most importantly, the call to accompaniment demands that bishops and religious superiors reject a clerical worldview that sees charges of clergy sexual abuse cast against a backdrop of status and immunities for those in the clerical state. Authentic Christ-like accompaniment sees all as equal in the Lord, and structures rooted in accompaniment make all feel and appear equal in the Lord.

Laity have been taught to put priests on pedestals and many have sustained them there. As we saw in chapter 3, some want to keep them there because in some ways it relieves the burden of being fully involved in the life and ministry of the Church. The major consequence of clericalism for the laity is passivity and dependence. "Lay clericalism is grounded in an immature dependence on clergy to mediate the believer's spirituality and relationship with God ... Lay clericalism enables the privileges and arrogance of the priesthood, trading adult negotiation of spirituality for ongoing clerical patronage/patronization."[24]

There is an associated pathology of hierarchicalism that must also be taken into account. In chapter 2 we saw that the special status of the priest facilitated the abuse. Special status and clerical narcissism are problematic when they are linked to political agendas and are not balanced by a strong servant ecclesiology witnessed by Jesus. Also, as we saw in chapter 2, clericalism diminished protection of children and youth in at least three ways:

> First, priest abusers and their superiors operated within an enclosed, self-protective clerical culture ... Second, priests moved from assignment to assignment without the open process of inquiry, interview, and evaluation that was characteristic of many other religious groups as well as professional appointments. Third, a powerful aura of being consecrated surrounded the Catholic priesthood....[25]

Church leadership strategies to avoid scandal also compromised their duty of protection.

Catholics are addicted to hierarchy. Not only do we establish a hierarchy for the Trinity – Father higher than Son and both higher than the forgotten Holy Spirit – but we have developed elaborate levels of status and authority that make most monarchies seem like flat organizations. The hierarchy of Pope – who is Pope *because* he is the Bishop of Rome, bishops, priests and laity becomes embellished by Cardinals and monsignors. There is even a priority of minor orders en route to priestly ordination. Some countries, such as Canada, have reintroduced the permanent diaconate, but co-opt deacons for cultic service at the altar and in some dioceses marginalize them from clergy study days. Despite the clear history of women deacons in the early Church, even many married permanent deacons are not in favour of recognizing them. We are tempted to clericalize all lay involvement in parish and other lay ecclesial ministries.

At the 2019 Summit, Sr. Veronica Openibo of Nigeria bluntly stated,

> Essential, surely, is a clear and balanced education and training about sexuality and boundaries in the seminaries and formation houses; in the ongoing formation of priests, religious men and women and bishops. It worries me when I see in Rome, and elsewhere, the youngest seminarians being treated as though they are more special than everyone else, thus encouraging them to assume, from the beginning of their training, exalted ideas about their status.

Renewing the theology, practice and formation for priests today as ministers of word, sacrament and service has been understood as crucial since the Second Vatican Council. A recent study has shown that formation for priesthood cannot occur in isolation, but within seminarians' relationship to the community and the mission shared by all the baptized.[26] The closed seminary as the modern site for forming clergy merits critical reflection for its role in promoting special status, power and clericalism.

The Church is a community for mission and "a sign and instrument of communion with God and of the unity among all peoples" (*Lumen Gentium*, no. 1). The mission of the Triune God, who is in constant mutual love, invites all the baptized to accept their call to be disciples. "There is no longer Jew or Greek, there is no longer slave or free, there is no longer male and female; for all of you are one in Christ Jesus" (Galatians 3:28). Ordination is neither a promotion beyond the ranks of the baptized nor an indicator of superior holiness. What is unique to ministers is their particular relationship to other members of the body of the Church. We need to eliminate from our discourse expressions such as "being reduced to the lay state" and "ceding authority to laity." New ways of clergy and laity working together are presented by the closure of parishes and a decline in priestly vocations in the global North. Necessity may help to overcome resistance to change and facilitate a return to the early Church's dependence on the gifts of all.

The role of women

Clericalism and patriarchy are inextricably linked in the Catholic Church. It can be very difficult to be a woman in the Church. This is especially true for educated and successful women who feel like second-class members. Secular research clearly indicates that the education and empowerment of women and girls is crucial to social change. Reports from the 2018 Synod on Youth and the working document for the 2019 Synod on the Amazon reveal that young women today have profound difficulty with the patriarchal Church and the role of women. The October 2018 Synod of Bishops concluded with a call for the inclusion of women in its all-male decision-making structures as "a duty of justice" that requires a "courageous change of culture."[27] The Summit participation dramatically showed women's contribution to honest, open and empathic conversation. Despite this, at the time of this writing there was news that the director, Lucetta Scaraffia, and all her Catholic female staff of a monthly magazine published by the Vatican's *L'Osservatore Romano* sent a letter of resignation to Pope Francis protesting the lack of support by the paper's new male editor, Andrea Monda.

Scripture, even though written by men, shows again and again Jesus' counter-cultural responses to women. His ministry undisputedly includes women. Many women followed him and supported his ministry; Mary of Magdala, Joanna and Susanna (Luke 8:1-3) followed him to the cross. Except for John, the men ran away. It was the women who stayed and saw where he was buried. Women were present at Pentecost and had public ministry in the early Church. Women had authority in the early Church.[28] They founded and led house church communities (Lydia, Prisca and Tabitha); taught male evangelists (Prisca) and took on the role of apostle in proclaiming the good news: Mary Magdalene, the first witness to the resurrection, is called "apostle to the apostles." Paul's earliest writings describe himself as an apostle, and Andronicus and Junia, a married missionary couple, "prominent among the apostles" (Romans 16:7).

Both Pope John Paul II and Pope Benedict XVI faced the question of women deacons. Both left the question for the magisterium to decide. In August 2016, Pope Francis created a Papal Commission of six men and six women, headed by Cardinal Luis Francisco Ladaria Ferrer of Spain, to study the specific role of women deacons in the early Church. In January 2019, before the Summit, Ferrer submitted the report to Pope Francis. It was not mentioned at the Summit. In May 2019, Pope Francis commented on the report's lack of consensus on the role of women deacons in the Church and stated that without this consensus, he could not move forward on an issue of sacramental ordination. For a Pope who is so committed to inclusion and justice, to shaking the Church from being a "stuffy museum of memories" and with a missionary impulse capable of changing everything for mission, his failure to read the signs of our times regarding the equality and interdependence of men and women is bewildering and profoundly discouraging.

Catholic feminists criticize scriptures written by males in a specific time and place.[29] Indeed, Jesus was male. But his notion of power would not be expected from a powerful male in his time. It would be expected from a woman. Feminists have concerns about Church interpretations of scripture based on ancient philosophical notions and anthropology. Aquinas and Bonaventure followed Aristotle in teaching that women do not have fully formed intellects or personhood. However, Jesus has many totally counter-cultural encounters with women in the scriptures. He is comfortable with them and had woman friends, including Martha and Mary. He treats them with respect. The apostles "were astonished that he was speaking with a woman" (John 4:27) when he has a conversation with the Samaritan woman at the well. He attends empathetically to those in need: the widow of Nain whose son has died, Jairus and his dying daughter, the widow who puts her penny into the treasury, and the woman taken in adultery. He says prostitutes will get into heaven before the righteous (Matthew 21:31). He refers to women in his parables: the woman mixing dough for bread (Matthew 13:33); the woman searching for a lost coin (Luke 15:8-10); the crippled woman who is bent over: "Woman, you are set free from your ailment" (Luke 13:12). He heals them and restores them to wholeness and to the community.

We saw in chapter 2 that the lack of insights from Catholic feminist philosophers and bioethicists' relational understanding of morality and sense of the harms of sins facilitated a focus on sins and offenders rather than on those harmed by the sins. Women are impoverished when their unique perspective is omitted from some areas of human life and discourse. Men, too, are less than they could be when they lose the insights of women. The Church as a whole is the poorer in a time when all resources are needed to overcome this tragic situation.

New ways forward

Pope Francis has recognized that

> It is impossible to think of a conversion of our activity as a Church that does not include the active participation of all the members of God's People ... whenever we have tried to

replace, or silence, or ignore, or reduce the People of God to small elites, we end up creating communities, projects, theological approaches, spiritualities and structures without roots, without memory, without faces, without bodies and ultimately, without lives.

This participation is not a kindly papal condescension but a right and duty of all the baptized. Nor is this participation for the sake of power itself.

In reflecting on Jesus and power, we saw that he washed his diciples' feet. We are challenged to figure out exactly what Jesus did in his example of servant leadership as we reform communities of the baptized for conversion and healing.

Pastoral pause and prayer

> ➤ What feelings arise in you when you reflect on the clergy sexual abuse crisis as abuse of power and authority in the Church?
> ➤ Have you personally experienced abuse of power in your parish or diocese?
> ➤ What are your thoughts on Jesus and his use of power?
> ➤ Are there practical implications here for your own parish or diocese?
> ➤ What could you do to help restore shared power and mutual recognition of the gifts of all?

Chapter 7

Infected by the Holy Spirit: An Ecclesiology for Healing and Renewal

When the day of Pentecost had come, they were all together in one place. And suddenly from heaven there came a sound like the rush of a violent wind, and it filled the entire house where they were sitting. Divided tongues, as of fire, appeared among them. All of them were filled with the Holy Spirit....
(Acts 2:1-4)

Introduction

In this book, we have seen that clergy sexual abuse is not only about horrific harm to the most vulnerable among us but is, in essence, an ecclesial crisis. Our interrogation of the history of the crisis and Church leadership led us to identify a list of personal and communal spiritual and organizational pathologies manifested in the crisis. We have experienced the difficulty in correctly diagnosing the crisis, polarizing diagnoses, and the harsh reality that misdiagnosing serious and life-threatening illness and providing symptomatic relief only lead to more suffering and even death. In the chapter 6 reflection on abuse of power, we acknowledged the need to reclaim the power of Jesus and his Holy Spirit for healing and renewal.

We have learned that much of our inability to identify and accept the deep pathology is rooted in beliefs and practices of the Church. So, here I again consult theology as an exercise of faith seeking understanding on the role of ecclesiology, the theology of the Church, in the crisis.

Dear Professor Deane,

What has been the role of ecclesiology in the long history of clergy sexual abuse and the inadequate leadership response? Why has the focus been on bureaucratic and technical responses to this spiritual and ecclesial crisis? How has the theology of episcopacy, priesthood and laity contributed to the hierarchical clerical culture? What might be the features of a new Spirit-filled ecclesiology needed for meaningful reform and healing?

Dear Sister Nuala,

In this consultation, I will respond to each of your four issues:

> *the role of ecclesiology in the crisis*
> *the reasons for the persistent focus on bureaucratic and technical responses*
> *the contributions of the theology of bishops, priesthood and laity to the crisis*
> *the features of a new Spirit-filled ecclesiology needed for meaningful conversion, reform and healing*

The role of ecclesiology in crisis

From debates about who among the apostles is the greatest (Mark 9:33-36) to the Pauline epistles, discussion about what the Church is and what it should be has been a feature of Christianity from the beginning. The theological discipline that concerns itself with the nature and structure of the Church is called ecclesiology. While always seeking to ground itself in scripture and Tradition, Catholic ecclesiology has evolved over time. This evolution has, at various stages, produced differing emphases. It is not that the Church understands itself through a very rigid model that a hundred years later is jettisoned, leading all Catholics to live and act in a wholly different way. Rather, subtle shifts in emphases shape how priests, bishops and lay people understand their roles. Metaphors and images come to dominate at certain times; sometimes these images of the Church have produced pathological results that need to be treated. In this section I will look at one very subtle but tremendously important attempt at such a treatment. I will argue that this treatment was needed to address a model of the Church that was pathological and fuelled many of the horrors visible in the sexual abuse crisis. This model it sought to correct, as I will explain, was marked by an understanding of the Church as a "perfect society," like developing nation-states, but "perfect." This understanding made it difficult to critique the Church and encouraged bishops to protect the Church's good name at the expense of victims. Similarly, it was a model in which clericalism, seen throughout this book as a major factor in sexual abuse, became rampant.

Lumen Gentium, the Dogmatic Constitution of the Church, was passed at the Second Vatican Council: the vote was 2,151 to 5. This kind of overwhelming majority isn't common in the Church. The practically unanimous support shows that the Council Fathers realized just how important it was to promulgate the ideas that *Lumen Gentium* offered, focused on empowering all the baptized and moving away from conflating the Church with a perfect society. Despite this massive majority, some splinter Catholic groups, such as the Society of Saint Pius X, see it as being heretical and marking an intolerable shift in the Church's ecclesiology. Why? *Lumen Gentium* reverses a "wartime" ecclesiology. As we saw in my reflections in chapter 5, the Protestant Reformation was followed by modernism, secularism and the growth of the nation-state. The Church saw all of these movements as threats, and began to understand itself as a city under siege. It started to see itself as a perfect society, assailed on all sides by dangerous and often evil forces.

This siege mentality was wholly understandable. Anyone who has spent any time reading Martin Luther's work knows just how vitriolic and visceral were his critiques of the Church. He sets a tone in the Reformation for understanding the Roman Church as not just sinful, but the whore of Babylon – corruption, sin and evil itself. The world the Reformation birthed was hostile to the Church and what it represented.[1] Tens of thousands of clergy were killed in the French Revolution. It was illegal in France for clergy to hold office well into the 19th century. Protestant countries like England saw Catholicism as the gateway of foreign hostile powers (such as Spain) into its very body. Germany under Bismarck engaged in a *Kulturkampf,* a cultural war wherein the emergent German nation-state sought to claim citizens' loyalty over and against the Church. Napoleon invaded the papal states and demanded that Pope Pius VI renounce all temporal power. When the Pope refused, he was taken to France under arrest, where he died one year later. The expression "wartime" ecclesiology, which I used earlier, is not an exaggeration.

The Church responded to this "war" aggressively. In the encyclical *Immortale Dei,* Leo XIII describes the Church as a "society" that "is supernatural … hence it is distinguished from civil society … and is a society chartered as of right divine, perfect in its nature" (no. 10). He situates the Church as a society in contrast to nation-states, distinguished from them by its divinely ordered perfection. The ecclesial emphasis was new in the Church. St. Augustine argued that the Church wasn't perfect – only Christ was. Aquinas knew this, and Dante's account of hell features plenty of popes and bishops. But this new ecclesial emphasis, seeing the Church as a "perfect society," develops dominance as the post-Reformation world wears on and the Church seeks to establish its uniqueness over and against Protestantism and new secular nation-states, which were claiming people's hearts and minds for themselves.

The emphasis on the Church as the "perfect society" was disastrous. The role it plays in the sexual abuse crisis is complicated but very important to understand. The Church contains many beautiful and holy things, in which Christ is present. So we love and serve the Church. But because we love the Church, we want it to become ever more the Body of Christ. And so we can and must critique it, looking to make it more Christ-like. Our core loyalty is to Christ; because of this, we love and serve the Church. Christ is perfect: we compare the Church to Christ, we see its imperfection, and we work to help it become ever more what it is called by Christ to be. Now, in contrast to this, let's say we assume the Church is perfect. It is not that we compare it to Christ, who is good itself. The Church, as perfect, is good itself. Therefore, any critique of the Church is a critique of goodness. Such critique is, by definition, evil.

The history and dynamics of clergy sexual abuse dramatically and tragically revealed this pathological ecclesiology at work again and again. Bishops saw the Church as perfect, as goodness itself. Because of this, it needed to be protected and preserved at all costs. Anything that could harm it was understood as evil. Therefore, as every report shows, the desire to avoid scandal and to protect the good name of the cleric and of the Church dominated the way allegations of sexual abuse were handled.

The Church was under siege – and not just metaphorically. The forces unleashed in the middle 300 years of the last millennium – the Reformation, the Enlightenment, the age of science, modernism and secularism – all led to an ecclesiology where the Church was understood as an ark, a pure, perfect society that was to be protected at all costs against the threats all around it. The victims of sexual abuse, then, rather than being seen as Christ himself, wounded and broken, were seen as threats. The goal, for bishops, was to silence them and protect the reputation of the perfect society under attack from all sides. This is just one very important example of how ecclesiology played a role in the sexual abuse crisis.

The Second Vatican Council sought to move away from this ecclesial emphasis. It offered an alternative ecclesiology in *Lumen Gentium*,[2] which understands the Church as "the people of God" and speaks of a "common priesthood of the faithful and the ministerial or hierarchical priesthood." These two forms of priesthood are "interrelated: each of them in its own special way is a participation in the one priesthood of Christ" (no. 10). *Lumen Gentium*, through the unself-conscious embrace of baptism as the instantiation of a "common priesthood," moves the Church beyond such an ecclesiological culture. Further, and even more radically, the Church, *Lumen Gentium* holds, as the people of God, "subsists in" (*subsistit in*) not "is" (*est*) the Roman Catholic Church. This has huge significance. As I noted above, the Church was seen as the ark of salvation, a perfect society in the midst of a world of sin hostile to it. With this simple term "subsist," *Lumen Gentium* does not just refuse this model: it goes so far as to say that the Church of Christ is broader than the Catholic Church. This may seem like a small thing today, but for centuries after the Reformation, it was unimaginable. "Subsist" is a difficult term to unpack, but without it we cannot appreciate how massive the move is away from the ecclesiology of a "perfect society."

So what does subsist mean? Well, the Holy Spirit subsists in your body. The Holy Spirit is inside you. You are not the Holy Spirit. Sometimes, when you billow with faith, hope and love, such as when you are in prayer, serving the poor or experiencing the sacraments, this presence of the Holy Spirit increases as you accept the Holy Spirit and union with Christ. Therefore, you "subsist" in the Holy Spirit to a great extent at these times. But again, you are not the Holy Spirit. The Holy Spirit is not you. So too, by using the language of "subsistence," *Lumen Gentium* holds that the Church is not always the Church of Christ. It can and does err. Sometimes it flows with the Spirit, and subsists in Christ more, but sometimes it acts, to use St. Paul's language, "according to the flesh." As Christ is broader than the Church, so too the Church of Christ, the people of God, are more than the Church. This is a truly radical rejection of the siege mentality ecclesiology of "perfect society," and it is why, for groups such as the Society of Saint Piux X, *Lumen Gentium* represents a heretical ecclesiology. The ecclesiology found in *Lumen Gentium*, supported by an overwhelming majority of 2,151 to 5 at the council, heralds a new age in the Church's self-understanding and puts behind it the "wartime" ecclesiology that existed since the Reformation.

Some might say Vatican II happened in the 1960s, but since much of the sexual abuse crisis played out in the decades that followed, the change in ecclesiology cannot have helped. But a pathological ecclesiology that evolved over 500 years cannot be wiped away in 50. The response to the Reformation began in the 16th century. Yet the "high point" of "perfect society" ecclesiology, as shown in Leo XIII's *Immortale Dei*, the declaration of papal infallibility and more, happened in the middle and latter part of the 19th century, 300 years later. So, too, the reforms begun at the Second Vatican Council will take longer than 50 years to permeate the cells of the Church.

The persistent bureaucratic and technical responses

A painful irony is that while the Church was trapped in a siege mentality marked by a "wartime ecclesiology," it was simultaneously incorporating many of the worst elements of the modern world that it sought to oppose. We have seen this already in the development of the Church as "perfect society." While most ecclesiological models, such as "the body of Christ" (used by Paul and the Church fathers), or "bride of Christ" (borrowed from Isaiah 62:5), are rooted in scripture or Tradition, the Church as "perfect society" is not. Its basis is the modern social order, from which the Church only differs, according to *Immortale Dei*, by virtue of its "supernatural foundation." Not scripture or Tradition but the secular nation-state provided the model from which this pathological ecclesiology grew. Just as it led to an ecclesial culture in which priest and bishops covered up sexual abuse to protect the good name of the "perfect society," other pathologies often seen in responses to this crisis can be found in modern secular culture.

One of these is bishops' reliance on bureaucracy and legislation rather than being present to the victims, as Christ would do. All reports on sexual abuse in the Church flag these forms of response; any worthwhile analysis needs to show how such pathologies developed. Only by identifying them can they be properly treated.

In this section I want to look at the origins of this emphasis on legalism and bureaucracy and to highlight how and when it became prevalent in the Church. As countless scholars have shown, the modern world is marked by a turn toward bureaucracy and legalism. Their analysis usually highlights the thought of German philosopher Immanuel Kant, who was especially influential. While many people have never heard of Kant, our politics and culture, and therefore our lives, are shaped his ideas. Two sources particularly produced his vision of the world. One was his background in a German piety, influenced by understandings of human depravity that came from the Reformer John Calvin. The other was a Scottish philosopher named David Hume who, Kant claimed, woke him from his "dogmatic slumber."[3] For Hume, we learn about the world through experience. We all have different experiences, so we will think differently about things like morality. Kant's problem was how to imagine a society in which we could avoid the moral relativism Hume's philosophy seemed to lead to, while also working with humans who, he thought (following Calvin), were inclined to depravity. In his 1795 highly influential essay "Perpetual Peace: A Philosophical Essay,"[4] Kant outlines such an approach. For him, the answer is to simply follow laws. So we establish laws, which human beings are inclined to break because they are weak and selfish. And so we make punishments. Humans, because they are weak and selfish, do not want to suffer these punishments, so they act as if they were virtuous, even though they are vice-filled!

Many of our societies work on this kind of approach. Rather than focus on shaping people to be morally good things who naturally desire the good, we make laws and establish punishments for those breaking the laws. This may seem tangential to the question at hand, but it is crucial: what Kant is doing here is rejecting the whole moral basis of Catholic Christianity. Catholic Christianity was never focused on laws. This doesn't mean that Christianity has not always had moral laws. What I mean is that, for the New Testament, the Church fathers, Aquinas and others, the moral life is not focused on controlling depraved people. It is focused on transforming people by the Holy Spirit. Not controlling bad people, but forming good ones. All people, within Catholic thought, can be conformed to Christ and transformed by the work of the Holy Spirit. This is the basis for the moral life, which Aquinas, for example, understands in terms of actions where we accept God's self-giving in the Holy Spirit.

This, of course, cannot be the basis for secular ethics. It is religious, and all religious perspectives are just that for Kant: perspectives. The moral framework for the state must be universal, not perspectival. That is why we need rational laws implemented by force. In this approach, the person's thoughts and feelings (some would say their humanity) are removed from the moral moment, and they simply implement the moral law.

Legalism has become incorporated into the Church's moral framework and ecclesial practices. Rather than resist the modern turn that we see in Enlightenment figures such as Kant, the Church increasingly comes to mirror the legalism of modernity. An obvious example is the way both liberals and conservatives will seek to use snippets of scripture as moral laws. While morality is understood – from Augustine to Aquinas and beyond – as an embodied embrace of God's self-giving, it becomes understood more and more as fealty to the laws of an arid distant deity.

For example, imagine that I am going into a store to buy myself something I don't need. Suppose there is a person in need at the door of the store. I hear the Holy Spirit; I know that God wants me to help that person. I know that God, in Christ, bound himself to the needy. In this moment God is seeking union with me, giving himself to me as the Spirit and wanting to conform me to the Son. If I say yes and give to the needy person, I am accepting "Christoformity" (being like Christ) through accepting the self-gift of the Holy Spirit. If I say no, I am saying no to being as Christ; I'm saying no to accepting the Holy Spirit who conforms me to Christ and enables me to act as Christ in the world. This is the kind of approach we see driving the theology of Augustine and Aquinas. In this approach, the person is shaped by their actions. The person receives or rejects the Holy Spirit in what they do. It is very different from thinking that God is in heaven, we are on earth, but if we follow God's laws we can appease God's wrath. The early lens is on the transformation of persons. It is about how people can become one with God and how the world can be changed through such people being in it.

The later lens is on keeping laws. A person is born with bad instincts; they live and die with them. But if they can overcome these instincts and follow God's laws, they can appease God's wrath and get to heaven. These two approaches are opposed. One sees union with God beginning in the world, and the moral life as the way of accepting this union. The other sees union with God as possible only after death; the moral life is about following laws to earn this union. The former represents the Church for most of its history; the latter comes into focus in the 18th century through figures like Kant.

And yet, in the modern world, legalist approaches become more common in the Church. The Church always had laws. It had codes of canon law, for example. There were a number of different codifications of laws or canons that governed Church habits and practices. They didn't govern the moral life. They were legalistic, governing Church regulations but not the moral life of people. Despite this, in the modern world we see two things: the compiling of all the different codes of canon law into one, to acknowledge its newfound importance; and the use of canon law not to guide structural habits in the Church, but in place of a moral framework.

It is only in 1917 that the Church centralizes the various codes of canon law. This brings about, to the modern mind, the advantages we have seen with Kant. It takes the person out of the equation. We can simply consult the law to know what to do. No personal circumstances can overwhelm the capacity of law and reason to shape best practice. But while anyone can see that dealing with a claim of sexual abuse is a profound moral moment, the reports show a Church marked by bureaucracy, using canon law to depersonalize the encounter. Bishops respond to victims not as wounded people who are dear to Christ, but by consulting laws, canonical and secular, that remove the bishop from the moral moment. The interactions are impersonal. The bishop, too often, disappears from the moral moment and takes solace in law. Too often he hands things over to secular law or aridly implements canon law.

Modern culture, as shaped by people like Kant, influences the Church as much as it does secular society. Just as modern Western culture holds that reason, technology and laws can save us, the Church also imbibes this arch-heresy by adopting legalism and bureaucracy as a surrogate for moral imagination.

To see the horror of this, we need only reflect on Mark 1:40-45, where Jesus heals a leper. The leper approaches Jesus and asks to be healed. Jesus is passionately moved to respond to the man's suffering. Jesus heals him and then tells the man not to tell anyone what had happened. Why, many Church fathers ask, does Jesus ask him for secrecy? Most assume that Jesus is on a mission: he is heading to Jerusalem for Passover, to be the lamb of the new Passover, to fulfill the scriptures and, literally, to save the world. But note, Jesus risks this. Jesus risks the salvation of the world because he is so moved by the leper's suffering. His response is not legalistic. It is personal, emotional, compassionate.

Two thousand years later, some of his followers responded to the needs of victims with the kinds of legalistic and bureaucratic approaches that were designed precisely to avoid this kind of personal reaction. The ecclesiological model, marked by bureaucracy, made it impossible for many bishops to respond *in persona Christi* to the needs of victims. Bishops should have seen the claims of victims as moments where they could accept the Holy Spirit and be one with Christ in their love of the victims. Instead of using such a framework, they took themselves out of the moral moment and hid behind the law, both canon and secular. This shows the colonization of the Church's moral imagination by approaches such as those we find in Kant.

Ecclesiology and the theology of episcopacy, priesthood and laity

The theology of episcopacy, priesthood and laity proceeds from St. Paul's understanding of life in Christ. He outlines this life in chapters 7 and 8 of his letter to the Romans. As an evangelist (Romans is a window into Paul's evangelical exhortations), he has a problem. His hearers do not consider the benefits he sees in a life in Christ as necessary. In following the law, his hearers think the world can be just and righteous. In Romans 7, Paul engages this supposition. He claims that even though he knows the law – even though he knows what he *should do* – he does not do it. The law is not enough. He knows the law, he knows the consequences, and yet he does not do what is good. Paul is, therefore, a problem to himself, and this problem cannot be solved through legislation.

The answer, for Paul, is that a human being can be transformed by the presence of the Holy Spirit in their mortal bodies. This transformation represents the Christian alternative to law alone. The indwelling of the Spirit, for Paul, changes the bodies of women and men. It fills them with gifts. As cream makes coffee different, the Holy Spirit, added to the "mortal bodies" (Romans 8:11) of women and men, changes their bodies in a very real sense. This process whereby the Spirit infused the body of men and women, conforming them to Christ, is, for Paul, the basis of the Church. The Church for Paul in Romans 8 is a people infused by the Holy Spirit who conforms them to Christ. It is the Body of Christ in the world, a pneumatological or Holy Spirit–filled community.

Such New Testament foundations for a Spirit-filled ecclesiology are maintained in an often overlooked section of the *Catechism of the Catholic Church*. The Church, the Catechism tells us, is Marian before it is Petrine (no. 773). Before there are buildings or even priests, there is the Church. It is present in the "yes" of a young woman to God's self-giving as the Holy Spirit. This self-giving leads to the presence of Christ within the Blessed Mother's body. This – Christ present in the bodies of women and men, through the Spirit – is the Church.

As noted in chapter 3, this indwelling of the Holy Spirit also binds us to each other. We are each part of Christ through the indwelling of the Spirit. The Spirit is one, Christ is one, the Father is one; therefore, when we are each part of God, we are one with each other. The Church is understood as this corporate body raised up through the indwelling of the Spirit in the bodies of women and men. As the Church begins at the annunciation, when the body of Mary receives the Holy Spirit, resulting in the presence of Christ within, our baptism is the moment when our union with the Holy Spirit is established: this is our incorporation into the Church.

In his letters Paul began this work, which later Church fathers build on. All who receive the Spirit become part of the Body of Christ. As Paul writes, "Now you are the body of Christ and individually members of it" (1 Corinthians 12:27). But this participation is not uniform. People receive different gifts, such as tongues, healing, preaching and teaching. Because of this, Paul often speaks about people as eyes, ears or hands (1 Corinthians 12:15): all different parts of one body.

Priests, like all other Christians, participate in the priesthood of Christ. But natural, sacerdotal gifts are illuminated by the Spirit. A priest's performance in the liturgy testifies to this. On Golgotha, God in Jesus Christ (true God) gives himself totally and without remainder to us. So too we in Jesus Christ (true human) give ourselves totally to God without remainder. This self-giving is the basis for an eternal union re-membered in the Eucharist. The Mass is therefore a calling to mind not simply of the Last Supper, but of Golgotha. The priest, as representative of the human Jesus, gives creation (the fruit of the vine and the work of human hands) back to God, accepting the union of God and creation in the bread and wine. Nothing, from the Catholic point of view, could be more significant or meaningful. And the priest, playing the role of Christ in this visible representation of the invisible life of the Trinity, is at its centre.

This, in Catholic ecclesiology, is the distinctive role of the priest. He performs in a dramatic re-presentation the Last Supper and the Passion – the Mass. His role is, properly understood, focused on this. His assumption of the role as "leader" – of prince in a parish principality – is something that has evolved in the culture but is *not* theologically mandated. The priest's role, theologically speaking, is significant, but also entirely circumspect. The elevation of the role of the priest to that of "professional Christian," who alone leads, alone preaches, alone visits the sick, feeds the hungry and decides on behalf of all – is not based on theology. It emerged over time and has been parasitic upon the life of the laity. The language we use to speak about the Church often imagines God as a kind of cosmic puppeteer. God chooses this person for that role and that person for another. This is a very human model, imagining God thinking and choosing the way we do. But when we look at the Church fathers, or Hildegard, for example, the images are more organic. The "perfect" Church would be one in which everyone acted in accordance with the will of the Spirit. No one would seek ordination to the priesthood without the gifts to carry out this role, and no one who had such gifts would be refused. No "perfect" Church would assume that because of such gifts, a priest would have gifts in teaching, preaching, pastoral care, decision making, leadership and on and on. The elevation of the role of priest to this role as "professional Christian" and "leader" is an ecclesial development with no theological basis. Of course, many priests are these things, but the conflation of the priesthood, over the last five centuries, with this "ministerial leader" role precludes others, not least women, from assuming this role.

In contrast, there is immense theological support in early Church sources for understanding the bishop as leader in the Church. But this form of leadership is distinctive; it should not be combined with the corporate managerial role bishops have assumed in the modern world. Bishops in the early Church were instruments of catholicity and unity. They were called to be conformed to Christ as chief priest and prophet, to preach, even to be martyrs. They were the radicals whom the Spirit conformed to Christ in very dramatic and visible ways. In early Christian documents, such as the letters of Ignatius of Antioch, or slightly later, as in the work of Justin Martyr, the bishop presided at the Eucharist and worked for the unity of the Church. Just as plants in a garden are distinct, bishops and priests have distinctive roles. The same sun and rain fall, but the plants grow in keeping with their nature. This garden has distinctive roles, but unlike the secular world, it is not a pyramid or a hierarchy. The lay person practising peace and justice is "being Church" and accepting Christoformity through the real presence of the Holy Spirit. The bishop is, too. The ways are different, but the process is the same.

The fact is, not every ordained priest or bishop has natural propensities toward liturgy or prophecy. An oak tree may find itself in an orchard, but no amount of sun or rain will lead it to produce an apple. An oak tree is not an apple tree, and even if the Church says it is, this does not make it so. The Holy Spirit builds on and perfects nature; it does not annihilate nature. Ordination builds on a vocation to the priesthood, but it can't give supernatural sacerdotal gifts to someone unless these gifts are latent within them. Otherwise, the Spirit would annihilate nature, which is alien to Catholic anthropology. Priesthood is common to all Christians. Prophecy, leadership and teaching are common to all Christians. But each person grows in accordance with nascent attributes that are inflamed by the Spirit and accepted in dramatic ways by our "yes" to the Spirit in the sacraments. The cultural conflation of the priesthood with Christian leadership must not continue to preclude the vast majority of Catholics from fulfilling their distinctive roles in the Church. Permeated by the Spirit, people's gifts serve Christ's body in the world. When Paul speaks of these gifts, he describes a vast array of gifts that in modern times have become the purview of clerics. The theological model offered here leaves no room for such a situation. If the Church is to be faithful to its own theology and Tradition, it must reform.

A renewed Spirit-filled ecclesiology for meaningful reform and healing

The dichotomy between lay and religious is, as we have seen throughout this book, pathological. What's more, it is alien to the core ecclesiology we see in scripture. The Second Vatican Council has begun to address this pathology. *Lumen Gentium*, looking to renew an early Christian ecclesiological model, stresses the shared participation in Christ that is central to all the people of God.

As we have seen throughout this consultation, the Council sought, once again, to see the Church as an ecosystem raised by the Spirit in accordance with diverse natures, rather than as a stratified bureaucracy. Over a half-century after *Lumen Gentium*, our ecclesiological culture is still changing.[5] The Church has had a tendency to mirror secular social orders – not through theology, but due to cultural evolution and layering. This mirroring was almost always at the cost of theological coherency and the work of the Holy Spirit. As noted above, the priest's role, theologically, focuses on the Mass. Yet priests have evolved to mirror leaders of secular organizations. Many bishops today also have a role that is more in keeping with an administrator or CEO than the role imagined for them in the theology of the Church.

The Spirit-filled ecclesiology we saw in the last section is one core aspect. The cultural layers through which the Church has mirrored secular models of organization and leadership is another. The horrific sexual abuse crisis has shown what happens when clergy understand their role as more protecting the brand than responding to the Spirit. This understanding was fuelled by an ecclesiology that saw the Church as a "perfect society." With one word – "subsist" – *Lumen Gentium* exploded that ecclesiological model. When the Church "subsists" in the Roman Catholic Church, when it abides in the Roman Catholic Church alongside much that is not the Church, the protection of all things Church as if it were Christ must be seen to be misplaced. With the word "subsist," *Lumen Gentium* frees priests and bishops to take risks, not least the kinds of risks that must be taken if the Spirit-filled ecclesiology invoked at the Council is to break through the layers of cultural calcification that have grown up around the Church.

By speaking about a "common priesthood," *Lumen Gentium*, and indeed the Second Vatican Council as a whole, sought to reignite the laity in the service of Christ's mission. The ecclesiology is clear: fuelled by baptism, Christians are capable of being conformed to Christ. This conformation to Christ is accepted in acts of teaching, prayer, preaching, healing and more – embodied actions that accept union with Christ, to whom such actions are natural. These actions are at once an acceptance of conformation to Christ and a clear sign of Christ's presence within us. This conformation works with our natures, our bodies and our souls to equip us to play roles within the Body of Christ. Episcopal roles, presiding, establishing unity and speaking prophetically; priestly roles, presiding at the Eucharist and sacraments; and many different roles, which Ignatius of Antioch calls "the business of Jesus Christ," that are performed by countless others: leading, teaching, healing, preaching, caring, decision making, serving, praying and more.

Relatively few roles in the life of the Church are best filled by priests or bishops. This is fitting, as there are very few priests and bishops relative to the 1.3 billion Catholics who make up the Church. But such an ecclesiology needs to emerge through layers of cultural practice, which impedes it. While the priest's role is focused on the Mass, the priest has become a professional Christian in a way that both protects lay people from their radical responsibility as followers of Christ and robs them of their rightful role as the people of God. Lay people, as much as priests, are called to be leaders. They are called to heal the sick, to visit the imprisoned, to feed the hungry. There is no theological basis for an emphasis on priestly primacy in all ecclesial decision making. Christ's priestly role is visible at the Last Supper and it is visible on Golgotha; to partake in this priestly identity is to partake in Christ, primarily in roles modelled on these moments. Christ as leader, administrator and decision maker are not, in theological history, aspects of Christ's priestly ministry.

Only if the Church takes risks, only if it trusts the Holy Spirit and its work in inspiring women and men, can the ecclesiology renewed at the Second Vatican Council once again govern how the Church lives and acts. The Church as "people of God," marked by a "common priesthood," needs to feel the weight of its 1.3 billion members. Any equation of the Church with the tiny minority of this number who are priests or bishops is a radical refusal to take seriously the ecclesiology promulgated at the Second Vatican Council. This ecclesiology, as this consultation has shown, consciously aimed to move the Church away from ecclesial emphases that have dogged it for centuries and played a pathological role in the sexual abuse crisis.

Dear Professor Deane,

This reflection on theological understandings of the Church has illuminated many of the pathologies manifested in the clergy sexual abuse crisis. It helps in linking beliefs about the Church directly to bureaucratic responses rather than to deep theological and spiritual conversion. You have elegantly highlighted, as we saw in chapter 5 that legalism and bureaucracy stifle moral imagination and conscience. The theology of the Church as the Body of Christ, with different parts having different roles, situates well theology of episcopacy, priesthood and laity needed today. Retrieving the Holy Spirit as essential in accepting the risks of conversion and reform is a powerful insight.

Pastoral pause and prayer

> ➤ How open are you to contributing your gifts to the Body of Christ in this day and age?
> ➤ Have you defaulted to legalism in your own moral life and failed to develop moral imagination and conscience?
> ➤ How open are you to the transforming power of the Holy Spirit?

Chapter 8

A Prescription for Conversion, Reform and Healing

"If you choose ... you can make me clean." Moved with pity, Jesus stretched out his hand and touched him, and said, "I do choose. Be made clean!" Immediately, the leprosy left him, and he was made clean." (Mark 1:40-43)

Introduction

Jesus' Paschal Mystery of suffering, death and resurrection to new life is the central mystery of our faith. In his Passion, he experienced the desire to deny and avoid pain and suffering: "Father," he prayed, "if you are willing, remove this cup from me" ... "In his anguish he prayed more earnestly, and his sweat became like great drops of blood falling down on the ground" (Luke 22:42-44). He knew feelings of loneliness and desolation: "I am deeply grieved, even to death" (Matthew 26:38), and "My God, my God, why have you forsaken me?" (Matthew 27:46). He surrendered to trust in God no matter how desperate things were: "'Father, into your hands I commend my spirit.' Having said this, he breathed his last" (Luke 23:46). And through his suffering and death, there is new life beyond imagining: "Why do you look for the living among the dead? He is not here, but has risen" (Luke 24:1-6).

At the closing Mass of the 2019 Summit, Archbishop Coleridge of Australia said,

> In these days we have been on Calvary … In the end, there remains only the voice of the Risen Lord, urging us not to stand gazing at the empty tomb, wondering in our perplexity what to do next … A mission stretches before us – a mission demanding not just words but real concrete action. If we can do this and more, we will not only know the peace of the Risen Lord but we will become his peace in a mission to the ends of the earth. Yet we will become the peace only if we become the sacrifice.

What sacrifice is required to make atonement for the harms and suffering of the clergy sexual abuse crisis?

For most patients, a serious, life-threatening illness or 'near-death' experience is a time of deep spiritual and moral meaning, a unique opportunity for an examination of conscience and life. In this book we have reflected upon the clergy sexual abuse crisis – the harming of children and youth – as an experience that must be accepted as a crucial turning point toward new life and possibility for all in the Church. We must act to assist victims and survivors in their healing and to ensure best practices in the Church for protection and prevention. However, a deep examination of conscience reveals that this abuse of the most vulnerable among us was allowed to occur as it has and for as long as it has *because* of deep-seated pathologies in the Church. Effective long-term prevention requires that we address these underlying endemic pathologies. Four related but distinct issues must be taken into account. The first is the centrality of repentance and meaningful atonement. The second relates to the spiritual challenge of responding to this crisis as disciples of Jesus. The third demands discernment of laws, organizational structures, relationships and policies of the institutional Church at every level that require repair. The fourth, and most difficult, element requires addressing polarizing and divisive diagnoses of some critical beliefs and practices in need of reform and repair.

Remember that the effectiveness of any prescription depends on the patient's recognition of their sickness and need for help, an accurate diagnosis, an effective and accessible treatment, and an accepting patient in a supportive environment. My goal in this final chapter is to assess the presence and power of these critical elements in any prescription for healing the Church from the long list of pathologies manifested in the clergy sexual abuse crisis.

Recognition of sickness and repentance as the first step in healing

"The time is fulfilled, and the kingdom of God has come near; repent, and believe in the good news." (Mark 1:15)

Recognition of our sickness and need for help is the first step in healing. Because the sickness revealed in the clergy sexual abuse crisis is a deep-seated personal and ecclesial sickness, this step requires prayerful examination of conscience and repentance. In his 2018 Letter to the People of God, Pope Francis invited "the entire holy faithful People of God to a penitential exercise of prayer and fasting, following the Lord's command. This can awaken our conscience and arouse our solidarity and commitment to a culture of care that says 'never again' to every form of abuse." At the Summit, Cardinal Gracias commented,

> To be the pilgrim people of God means that we are a community that is called to continuous repentance and continuous discernment. We must repent – and do so together, collegially – because along the way we have failed. We need to seek pardon. We must also be in a process of continuous discernment … We have come to know that there is no easy or quick solution. We are summoned to move forward step by step and together. That requires discernment.

The pilgrimage described here is not one in the security and safety of a modern tour bus with all the amenities, but one like those of early Christian pilgrims risking life and enduring hardship on the holy journey, or today's homeless migrants seeking safety and peace.

In invoking the Great Jubilee of the Year 2000, Pope John Paul II focused on the Church taking responsibility for past faults of her sons and daughters and making amends. The International Theological Commission, under then Cardinal Ratzinger, studied the question and concluded that "Indeed, in the entire history of the church there are no precedents for requests for forgiveness by the magisterium for past wrongs."[1] In the recent past and in dramatic ways at the Summit, the Church has made many apologies for the clergy sexual abuse crisis.

Apologies have become politically correct crisis risk management strategies in secular organizations. A normative standard for apologizing requires it to be performed in an appropriate context and to explicitly acknowledge wrongdoing, accept responsibility, express regret, identify with those harmed, fully disclose, provide explanation and offer corrective action.[2] For followers of Christ, sorrow for our sins and failings is no mere politically correct public relations strategy. It requires a rending of our hearts and a conversion of our lives. In the sacrament of reconciliation, we acknowledge and confess our sins and failings, accept a penance and commit to making amends. Atonement is an essential requirement for forgiveness. Church leadership must now model and facilitate practical and effective penance and meaningful atonement. Repentance demands examination of conscience. Hinze proposes that

> Changes in discourse and actions is the basic ingredient in any act of conversion. If the sinfulness of the Church is solely a matter of the sins of individuals, then it is individuals who must change. But if the sinfulness of the Church is a matter of collective, institutional responsibility, do not the Church's doctrines and practices need to be changed in order for the penitential process to be complete? In other words, are there

instances when ecclesial repentance can and should serve as a catalyst for doctrinal change?[3]

Because the pathologies manifested in the abuse crisis are endemic, widespread and multi-generational, the Church needs help in seeing and accepting them. Many of the pathologies have become so normalized that they cannot be recognized. In chapter 2, studies on organizational moral failure revealed many factors creating a toxic environment for the Church, particularly its hierarchical nature and clericalism, secrecy and lack of participation in decision making by the laity, and active discouragement of opportunities for dialogue and sense-making of the crisis. A sole focus on laws, policies and bureaucratic practices, rather than on the virtues and practices that promote conversion, dialogue, mutual accountability, moral sensitivity and courage, has resulted in persistent misdiagnosis of the underlying pathologies. All misdiagnosis results in prolonged and progressive pain and suffering.

We have seen that, for many, a theology of the Church as the "perfect society" has prevented them from recognizing or accepting the need for continuous personal and ecclesial conversion and structural reform. Reform of structures is essential, but it requires deeper spiritual conversion so that structures and policies support mission. Clearly, "the Church is not to be deduced from her organization; the organization is to be understood from the Church."[4] Church structures are authentic to the degree that they serve mission. We must take into account all of the identified pathologies in the lived experience of the Church and open the way to treatment and prevention in a Church that is badly wounded by the global crisis but debilitated in responding from endemic pathology.[5] The conversion and reform necessary for healing require what Pope Francis calls in *Evangelii Gaudium* "a missionary impulse capable of transforming everything, so that the Church's customs, ways of doing things, times and schedules, language and structures, can be suitably channeled for the evangelization of today's world rather than for her self-preservation!" (no. 27).

Forty years after the public revelations of this long-standing issue, we still have denial from some clergy and laity that this is an ecclesial crisis. In chapter 3, we reviewed the irreconcilable differences and polarizing diagnoses that are fracturing the unity of the Church and paralyzing response, including accusations of heresy against Pope Francis himself. The dissension and division have been raised to new heights in the unfortunate 2019 letter of former Pope Benedict.

They are a clear sign of pathology in the Body of Christ.

The spiritual challenge of responding to the crisis as disciples of Christ

"Let the same mind be in you that was in Christ Jesus."
(Philippians 2:5)

The abuse crisis demonstrates a Church in need of personal and ecclesial spiritual conversion to "the mind of Christ" and a reformation to discipleship through the power of the Holy Spirit. As we were reminded in our theology consultation in chapter 5, this continual reformation is not optional. It is an absolute, not simply a socio-historical phenomenon. As Pope Francis reminds us, the Church is not an ideology; it is a call to discipleship. This formation requires first and foremost an ongoing spiritual conversion that is then supported by the construction of doctrinal, legislation and systemic supports.

Pope John Paul II, whose papacy covered the modern crisis from its earliest revelations and established the pattern of leadership response, held heroic notions of priesthood. He had great difficulty with clergy sexual abuse, but at the end of his life came to understand that "Sexual abuse within the Church is a profound contradiction of the teaching and witness of Christ."[6] In his 2010 Christmas greeting to the Curia, Pope Benedict declared,

We must accept this humiliation as an exhortation to truth and a call to renewal. Only the truth saves. We must ask ourselves what we can do to repair as much as possible the injustice that has occurred. We must ask ourselves what was wrong in our proclamation, in our whole way of living the Christian life, to allow such a thing to happen.[7]

Pope Francis posits discipleship requiring continual conversion to "the mind of Christ" as essential for the Body of Christ to be healed from the pathologies manifested in the crisis. In his 2018 Letter to the People of God, Pope Francis wrote,

> every one of the baptized should feel involved in the ecclesial and social change that we so greatly need. This change calls for a personal and communal conversion that makes us see things as the Lord does ... To see things as the Lord does, to be where the Lord wants us to be, to experience a conversion of heart in his presence.

The history provided in chapter 1 identified the features of Church leadership response to victims and the global crisis. Each of these must be now be assessed spiritually, theologically and structurally and reformed in ways conforming to the "mind of Christ":

- Abuse of power, trust and sacred office must be transformed to Jesus' understanding and exercise of power: *"learn from me; for I am gentle and humble in heart"* (Matthew 11:29).
- Insensitivity to the physical, psychological and spiritual harm to vulnerable children and youth must be transformed by Jesus' love of children, *"Let the little children come to me"* (Mark 10:14), and outrage at their abuse: *"it would be better for you if a great millstone were fastened around your neck and you were drowned in the depth of the sea"* (Matthew 18:6).
- Secrecy, silence and denial, including intentional cover-up, must recognize that *"nothing is covered up that will not be uncovered, and nothing secret that will not become known"* (Matthew 10:26-28).

> ➤ Preferential protection of offenders and Institution to avoid scandal needs to accept Jesus' condemnation of hypocrites as *"whitewashed tombs, which on the outside look beautiful, but inside they are full of the bones of the dead and of all kinds of filth"* (Matthew 23:27).

> ➤ Divisive and polarizing assessments of the underlying pathology and its treatment need to listen to Jesus' prayer: *"I ask not only on behalf of these, but also on behalf of those who will believe in me through their word, that they may all be one. As you, Father, are in me and I am in you, may they also be in us, so that the world may believe that you have sent me"* (John 17:20-21).

Unless we are personally and collectively rooted in the "mind of Christ," we will be constantly at risk of creating new pathologies of power and privilege.

Discerning reforms for effective treatment and healing

Discernment regarding the transformation of structures, policies and practices with the "mind of Christ" is crucial so as to not enshrine new pathologies of nostalgic restorationism or democratizing the Church. Discernment requires "humility, discretion, and love for the church and her teaching, in a sincere search for God's will and a desire to make a more perfect response to it."[8] Not surprisingly, the Jesuit Pope Francis has emphasized the importance of discernment, a centuries-old process that invites individuals into a profound personal experience of God that evokes a deep life conversion and a renewed sense of mission. It relies on scripture, Tradition, experience and science to help ponder the principles, images and ideas that guide us. It requires us to use our imagination to place ourselves with Jesus in the scriptures and learn "the mind of Christ". In discernment we can experience both spiritual consolation and desolation. In a very real sense, the Church today is experiencing spiritual desolation. From this place, the whole People of God need to discern together where the Holy Spirit is calling us. Pope Francis and others have cautioned that discernment takes time and guidance.

However, just as the health care team must urgently address the breathing and heartbeat of a patient who is experiencing a heart attack before investigating its causes and consequences, there is need for some urgent action here to protect life and health. The most urgent need is for the Church to ensure protection of the vulnerable. This protection requires a preferential option for victims, their families and communities rather than for offenders and the Church's reputation. Dioceses must accompany, protect and treat victims, offering them support for healing. On May 9, 2019, Pope Francis's Apostolic Letter "Vos Estis Lux Mundi" finally mandated every diocese in the world to create concrete procedures for reporting the sexual abuse of minors, child pornography, and abuse of others such as seminarians, religious women and lay women, with the letter entering into force on June 1, 2019. It recognized that clergy sexual abuse has many victims. The letter creates a new process for metropolitan archbishops to have the authority to investigate bishops who are guilty of abuse or the cover-up of abuse.

Bishops must also share best practices and identify individuals or groups that are easily accessible to victims. Such people or groups should have some autonomy when it comes to oversight. There must be education programs for clergy and laity to form a shared understanding of an acceptable code of conduct for all. Sexual abuse of minors is not only a sin but a crime in most nations. A member of the clergy – priest or bishop – who commits this crime or fails to act to protect children and youth must be prosecuted to the full extent of canon and civil law. Periodic reviews of protocols and norms are needed to ensure that the Church's action in this matter conforms with her mission. This is a major advance. However, the failure to recognize the need for lay participation in investigation and oversight is a serious flaw. Powerful groups with public duties and responsibilities, such as medicine, have learned they cannot adequately monitor themselves.

There is also an urgent need for the Church to reclaim credibility as an agent of justice and care that will act to deal with all pathologies in this crisis. We saw insights from the literature on organizational moral failure in chapter 5 that this requires a cultural transformation for the organization in which the moral failure occurred. These insights recognize that changing a culture that fostered the failure is far more difficult than creating a new culture. Key to this transformation is definitive action demonstrating the new philosophy and culture. So, there is also an urgent need to dismantle clericalism, hierarchy and patriarchy, but this will not be easy. Some radical surgery may be needed.

An important factor in demonstrating this cultural transformation and regaining public credibility is the setting of new directions and policies. The Church now needs to send some dramatic signs of a new culture that do not require further discernment when it comes to changes in doctrine or revision of canon law. Some bold moves that would clearly signal the Church's commitment to a new way of being a Church of disciples of Christ might include the following:

> the appointment of lay women and men to the College of Cardinals, which would demonstrate a new partnership of clergy and laity together in mission

> the elimination of mandatory celibacy for priests of the Latin Rite, which would not only overcome the present confusion (all other Catholic Rites have married clergy) but remove one of the elements creating a special status for priests as holier than laity

> resolve the lack of unanimity in the report on women deacons by "reading the signs of the times" and rejecting patriarchy

> require the participation of laity in investigation and oversight of clergy sexual abuse allegations and leadership response

- ‣ address as an urgent issue the formation of priests and role of the closed seminary environment in clericalism and patriarchy
- ‣ mandate teaching for clergy and laity alike regarding the revered tradition of formation of conscience needed for discernment.

We have reflected on the critical importance of moving forward with the "mind of Christ" and the power of the Holy Spirit, and on acknowledging the need for repentance and atonement. In addition, the principles in the 2018 Canadian Conference of Catholic Bishops' document *Protecting Minors from Sexual Abuse* – responsibility, accountability and transparency – which were used to organize the 2019 Summit in Rome, can help focus on practical changes. These changes are necessary to develop and foster a new culture in the Church.

We need a culture not only for Church leadership responsibility but for *co-responsibility* of the whole people of God for the healing and reconciling ministry of Jesus. This demands an ecclesiology that promotes and privileges the priesthood of all the baptized and the theology of the gifts of all. Clericalism is an elitist contradiction to the radical equality of the baptized. We need to reclaim the participation of all in the one priesthood of the baptized, with rights and responsibilities. Clearly, there are distinctive gifts and roles within the Church. These are not for power and privilege, but for mission. Moreover, as *Lumen Gentium* noted, "For the distinction which the Lord made between sacred ministers and the rest of the People of God bears within it a certain union, since pastors and the other faithful are bound to each other by a mutual need" (no. 32).

Theology of priesthood needs revision, with particular attention to special status and power being converted to Jesus' servant leadership. Renewal of seminary formation is crucial.[9] In chapter 6 we identified a pre-Summit report on seminary formation and priesthood with key insights for clergy and laity moving forward together.[10]

We don't have to create a role for the laity. The understanding of the Church as the Body of Christ, where every part has its role in the life and health of the whole, is clear. What is needed is to walk the talk of our theology to ensure meaningful, not just consultative, involvement of the laity, both men and women, in decision making, the development of doctrine, and oversight. In light of all formal authority and teaching from males, there is a paradoxical conservative pushback against what they call a "feminized Church." This needs deeper reflection.

Organizational structures, policies and relationships at every level need reform. At the highest level, Pope Francis has emphasized the need for a new synodality, a journeying together, listening and dialoging in charity. The Synod on Youth demonstrated a new way of listening, to hear the hopes and concerns of youth, not just to listen and respond with traditional teaching. Pope Francis's reform of the Roman curia in *Praedicate Evangelium* puts a priority on evangelization and synodality. It consolidates dicasteries in Rome and puts them at the service of both the Pope and bishops. This represents a major cultural shift at the highest level.

The Pontifical Commission for the Protection of Minors has been confirmed as an independent institution connected to the Holy See with an advisory function for the Holy Father. Originally, it was intended for policy change: "to propose initiatives to the Roman Pontiff ... for the purposes of promoting local responsibility in the particular Churches for the protection of all minors and vulnerable adults." It has done important work in education, protection and safeguarding initiatives despite limited resources and opposition.

National bishops' conferences, dioceses and parishes also need cultural transformation. An excellent example of a plan for this transformation in the US Church has been developed by the Catholic Partnership 2019 Leadership Roundtable, in its report *Heal the Body of Christ*.[11] Finally, diocesan reorganization, with the closure and merging of parishes that is occurring throughout the global North, presents a graced opportunity to respond in ways that are truly compatible with co-responsibility and accountability. Necessity requires a new way of using the gifts of all and new ways of dialogue and decision making which can transform communities of faith to be more like the early Church.

A culture of co-responsibility requires a moral theology that retrieves and renews venerable Church teaching on conscience. Chapter 2's reflection on the role of moral theology in the crisis calls for urgent attention to formation of conscience and the cultivation of virtues.

A culture of accountability for our gifts and our responsibilities is an essential complement to co-responsibility. This requires the promotion and support of communication and dialogue in the Church to counteract the secrecy and denial that have dominated the crisis. This requires both speaking and listening to each other in contrast to the constricted notions of a "teaching Church" of the clergy and a "listening Church" of the laity. This will call for meaningful consultation with laity and their participation in decision making. It will allow the laity and the clergy together to have opportunities for making sense of tragedies such as clergy sexual abuse.

A culture of transparency is essential to combat the silence, secrecy and denial that characterize all abuse of power and position, particularly sexual abuse. Transparent and effective mechanisms for holding leadership accountable are needed at every level. This requires a transformation of the Church's culture of management, from self-protection and avoidance of scandal – narrowly understood as reputational loss – to humble accountability for carrying on Jesus' mission in a wounded world.

Throughout this book, experts in a number of fields of inquiry have raised issues related to beliefs and doctrines in need of conversion and reform. All of these need discernment and careful spiritual and theological analysis, which is beyond the scope of this work. This is not just apologetics, repeating more forcefully traditional teaching. This is the task of putting the new wine of the new evangelization in new wineskins of relationships, communication and structures.

Challenges for theology are a crucial element in the unfinished work of conversion and healing.

New paths of dialogue between academic theologians and the Magisterium must be paved. Massimo Faggioli's talk at the June 2019 conference of the Catholic Theological Society of America identifies this challenge, with particular attention to polarization and extremization of views most dramatically demonstrated around liturgical reform.[12]

In March 2020, the Pontifical Gregorian University Centre for Child Protection will host an invited laboratory on "Doing Theology in the Face of Sexual Abuse" to address issues of justice to victims, perpetrators and the entire Church; ecclesiologies that help us rediscover Jesus; priesthood as service and rejection of clericalism; sexuality and the mission of the Church.[13]

There is also need for attention to insights from science and evolutionary theory in the New Cosmology. Further study of Christian anthropology in light of advances in science is essential in reforming and renewing our theology of sexuality and in our understanding of women in the modern world. Serious reflection on sex and gender issues must take into account scientific advances as well as address the discrimination and exclusion against persons with sexual differences in a faith where an essential belief is the inherent dignity of all persons.

My diagnosis has focused on conversion to "the mind of Christ." It has been informed and inspired by the gospels. Many feminist scholars have raised concerns about the scriptures and their patriarchal background. My reflections see Jesus as profoundly counter-cultural regarding women – not only for his time, but in contrast to Church teaching and practice from the third century to today. Scriptural theology is also in need of renewal.

Supportive environment

Even with a correct diagnosis, healing requires an accepting patient in a supportive environment. As we saw earlier, Pope Francis uses a medical metaphor to capture the environment in which we try to respond to the challenges of the abuse crisis: "I see the church as a field hospital after battle … You have to heal [the] wounds. Then we can talk about everything else. Heal the wounds." The Church is not responding to the clergy abuse crisis from a position of strength, but one of a long period of decline in technologically developed and secular nations and of socio-cultural changes.[14] The loss of the transcendent for many, the rise of the "nones" – people with no religious affiliation or participation, especially among the young – and atheism raise deep questions about the future of religion. This is the focus of a May 2019 conference at the Pontifical Gregorian University on "Understanding Unbelief." The presence of deep divisions about diagnosis and treatment in the Church has created a difficult environment to support healing, especially in secular commercialized and technologically dependent societies which have lost the sense of transcendence.

Thoughts on prognosis

Do you not know all of us who have been baptized into Christ Jesus were baptized into his death? Therefore we have been buried with him by baptism into death, so that, just as Christ was raised from the dead by the glory of the Father, so we too walk in newness of life. For if we have been united with him in a death like his, we will certainly be united with him in a resurrection like his. (Romans 6:3-5)

In our technologically dependent society, we demand a quick fix for any and all of our distress. There is no quick-fix drug or device to address the pathologies manifested in the clergy sexual abuse crisis. The profound pain and suffering to the Body of Christ from this crisis demands deep conversion and reformation to a Church of disciples of Jesus Christ who are courageous in speaking truth to power and protecting the vulnerable. Deep conversion in the Church, along with real structural reform, is required to build resilience to withstand future infection and disease and to heal from this dark night of the Church's soul.

Patients who are sick are concerned with very basic questions: "What is wrong with me?" "What is the treatment?" "Can you fix it?" "Am I going to die?" Giving a prognosis about outcome is the most risky of all medical acts, even with a correct diagnosis and available effective treatment.

I have loved and prayed for Pope Francis from the moment he stepped out onto the balcony in Rome, greeted the crowds, and bowed his head for their blessing before he gave them his own. He has been a witness to care and concern for the vulnerable and those on the peripheries. He has also provided brilliant diagnoses of many of the pathologies in his identifying the temptations of the Church and diseases of leadership. He has made it clear that conversion of mind and heart should precede structural change. He has called for a missionary impulse that can change "everything" for the new evangelization and mission. In light of the global crisis of the Church mortally wounding some and paralyzing others, I am bewildered and disappointed at his inaction on some crucial issues that he could change. He needs to walk the talk, particularly the concern for the vulnerable, the role of women in the Church and the importance of dialogue and discernment. The Church needs dramatic action following the 2019 Summit, where brave and honest things were said. It needs action while Francis is still Pope because the resistance to conversion and reform is powerfully present in the Church.

There are other challenges to healing. Church leaders are manifesting a 'tragedy fatigue' which is well known in field hospitals and other situations of ongoing crisis. The silence of the clergy and their difficulty in sharing their pain with others is a significant impediment to healing. Remember Fr. Donald Cozzens's observation from chapter 4 on silence and denial: "what really scandalizes countless numbers of the faithful is the church's readiness – tragically exemplified in recent decades by its response to the sexual misconduct cases involving a significant number of priests and bishops – to deny and minimize the depth, scope, and pastoral implications of issues that cry out for analysis and action."[15] We cannot minimize the harm and pastoral implications of the clergy sexual abuse crisis.

My prognosis for conversion, healing and repair is determined by my belief in the power of the Resurrection. Human institutions and organizations have a natural life cycle. After crisis, many will die out; some need to. Others return to the true foundation and reform and renew. The Church as the Body of Christ is a Resurrection people. We may be in a Calvary time of desolation and pain, but we know that our Redeemer lives. If only we can turn to the Lord and trust in him.

"Lord, save us! We are perishing!" And [Jesus] said to them,
"Why are you afraid, you of little faith?" (Matthew 8:25-26)

Prayer for the Future

God of love, you gave your only Son to save us by his blood on
  the cross.
Join to your Son's suffering the pain of all who have been hurt in
  body, mind and spirit
by those who betrayed the trust placed in them.
Hear the cries of our brothers and sisters who have been gravely
  harmed,
and grant them justice and healing,
through our participation in the work of the Holy Spirit.

We pray for atonement and healing as we acknowledge the hurt,
  anger and shame
our Church has experienced through the sexual abuse of children
  and vulnerable adults.
We confess the profound damage done to the proclamation of
  Christ's gospel in our homes, parishes and communities.
We place before God's healing love the innocent ones
and before God's judgment those guilty of misusing their power.

For the crimes and sins of sexual and physical abuse perpetrated by
  clergy and servants of the Church against children and young
  people; for the failure to respect, nurture and cherish young
  people – especially the most vulnerable.

For the immense psychological harm and lasting spiritual devastation caused to survivors of abuse by Church representatives.

For the failure of bishops when they did not respond as good and
  compassionate shepherds to victims of abuse by priests. For
  the practice of covering up crimes of abuse that caused more

instances of sexual abuse; for the scandal caused in the hearts and minds of the faithful.

For the sins of those clergy who not only abused God's children, but abuse God's people by failing to carry out their pastoral responsibilities.

For the anguish and distress caused to the families and friends of those abused. For the burdens they carry and the injuries inflicted on their loved ones.

For those who died prematurely or who took their own lives as a consequence of the spiritual, psychological and emotional damage they suffered through abuse.

Heavenly Father,
In every age, you have been our refuge.
Yet again and still, we stand before you
asking for protection on your Church, with all her strengths and weaknesses.

May Jesus, our High Priest and the Church's one foundation,
continue to lead his Church in every thought and action of his disciples,
that through him, our Church can be an instrument of justice,
a source of consolation,
   a sacrament of unity,
   and a manifestation of the good news of healing and reconciliation.

May the Holy Spirit fill the hearts of the faithful
that we may renew the face and Body of the Church.
We ask this through Christ our Lord.
Amen.

Endnotes

Introduction

1   All papal and magisterial documents, unless otherwise referenced, are found on the Zenit website: https://zenit.org.

2   Nuala Kenny, *Healing the Church: Diagnosing and Treating the Clergy Sexual Abuse Crisis* (Toronto: Novalis, 2012).

3   Antonio Spadaro, S.J., "A Big Heart Open to God: An Interview with Pope Francis," *America*, September 30, 2013, http://americamagazine.org/pope-interview.

4   C. Colt Anderson, "Bonaventure and the Sin of the Church," *Theological Studies* 63 (2002): 677–89 at 675.

5   Paul D. Murray, "Searching the Living Truth of the Church in Practice: On the Transformative Task of Systematic Theology," *Modern Theology* 30:2 (2014): 251–81 at 267.

Chapter 1

1   International Theological Commission, "Memory and Reconciliation: The Church and the Faults of the Past," *Origins* 29:39 (March 16, 2000): 625–44.

2   Thomas P. Doyle, A.W. Richard Sipe and Patrick J. Wall, *Sex, Priests, and Secret Codes: The Catholic Church's 2000-Year Paper Trail of Sexual Abuse* (Los Angeles: Volt Press, 2006).

3   C. Colt Anderson, "When Magisterium Becomes Imperium: Peter Damian on the Accountability of Bishops for Scandal," *Theological Studies* 65 (2014): 741–66.

4   Timothy D. Lytton, *Holding Bishops Accountable: How Lawsuits Helped the Catholic Church Confront Clergy Sexual Abuse* (Cambridge, MA: Harvard University Press, 2008); James T. O'Reilly and Margaret S.P. Chalmers, *The Clergy Sex Abuse Crisis and the Legal Response* (New York: Oxford University Press, 2014).

5   David E. DeCosse, "Freedom of the Press and Catholic Social Thought: Reflections on the Sexual Abuse Scandal in the Catholic Church in the United States," *Theological Studies* 68 (2007): 865–99.

6   The Editors, "Priest Child Abuse Cases Victimizing Families; Bishops Lack Policy Response," *National Catholic Reporter*, June 7, 1985.

7   F. Ray Mouton, Thomas P. Doyle and Michael R. Peterson, "The Problem of Sexual Molestation by Roman Catholic Clergy: Meeting the Problem in a Comprehensive and Responsible Manner," BishopAccountability.org, June 8-9, 1985.

8   Special Archdiocesan Commission of Inquiry (Gordon A. Winter, Nuala P. Kenny, Everett MacNeil, Frances G. O'Flaherty and John A. Scott), *The Report of the Archdiocesan Commission of Enquiry into the Sexual Abuse of Children by Members of the Clergy: Conclusions and Recommendations*, 2 vols. (St. John's, NL: Archdiocese of St. John's, 1990), 91.

9   Canadian Conference of Catholic Bishops, *From Pain to Hope* (Ottawa: Publications Service, 1992).

10   United States Conference of Catholic Bishops, *The Five Principles to Follow in Dealing with Accusations of Sexual Abuse* (Washington, DC: USCCB Office of Media Relations, 1992).

11   United States Conference of Catholic Bishops, *Charter for the Protection of Children and Young People* (Washington, DC: United States Conference of Catholic Bishops, 2002).

12   The Investigative Staff of the Boston Globe, *Betrayal: The Crisis in the Catholic Church* (Boston: Back Bay Books, 2002).

13   National Review Board for the Protection of Children and Young People, *A Report on the Crisis in the Catholic Church in the United States* (Washington, DC: United States Conference of Catholic Bishops, 2004).

14   John Jay College of Criminal Justice, Catholic Church and United States Conference of Catholic Bishops, *The Nature and Scope of Sexual Abuse of Minors by Catholic Priests and Deacons in the United States, 1950–2002* (Washington, DC: United States Conference of Catholic Bishops, 2004); John Jay College of Criminal Justice, *The Causes and Context of Sexual Abuse of Minors by Catholic Priests in the United States, 1950–2010* (Washington, DC: United States Conference of Catholic Bishops, 2011).

15   Gregory Erlandson and Matthew Bunson, *Pope Benedict XVI and the Sexual Abuse Crisis: Working for Reform and Renewal* (Huntington, IN: Our Sunday Visitor Publishing Division, 2010).

16   Pastoral Letter of the Holy Father Pope Benedict XVI to the Catholics of Ireland (2010), http://w2.vatican.va/content/benedict-xvi/en/letters/2010/documents/hf_ben-xvi_let_20100319_church-ireland.html.

17   Benedict XVI, Address of His Holiness Benedict XVI on the Occasion of Christmas Greetings to the Roman Curia, Libreria Editrice Vaticana, December 20, 2010.

18   Yvonne Murphy, Ita Mangan and Hugh O'Neill, *Report by Commission of Investigation into Catholic Archdiocese of Dublin* (Ireland: Department of Justice and Equality, 2009), 15.

19   Royal Commission into Institutional Responses to Child Sexual Abuse, *Final Report: Religious Institutions* 16, Book 1 (Commonwealth of Australia: Attorney General's Department, 2017), 36.

20   Nichoals P. Cafardi, *Before Dallas: The U.S. Bishops' Response to Clergy Sexual Abuse of Children* (Mahwah, NJ: Paulist Press, 2008).

21   Katarina Schuth, *Seminary Formation: Recent History, Current Circumstances, New Directions* (Collegeville, MN: Liturgical Press, 2016).

22   Thomas P. Doyle, "Clericalism: Enabler of Clergy Sexual Abuse," *Pastoral Psychology* 54:3 (2006): 189–213 at 201.

23   Elise Harris, "Abuse Survivor Resigns from Commission for Protection of Minors," Catholic News Agency, March 1, 2017, https://www.catholicnewsagency.com/news/abuse-survivor-resigns-from-commission-for-protection-of-minors-45510.

24   "Cardinal O'Malley: Pope Caused 'Great Pain' for Abuse Survivors in Chile," *National Catholic Reporter*, January 20, 2018, https://www.ncronline.org/news/vatican/cardinal-omalley-popes-defense-chilean-bishop-caused-great-pain-abuse-survivors.

25   "Full text of Pope Francis' letter to the Church in Chile," Catholic News Agency, June 5, 2018, https://www.catholicnewsagency.com/news/full-text-of-pope-francis-letter-to-the-church-in-chile-35580.

26   Junno Arocho Esteves, "Pope apologizes for 'serious mistakes' in judging Chilean abuse cases," Catholic News Service, April 11, 2018, https://www.catholicnews.com/services/englishnews/2018/pope-apologizes-for-serious-mistakes-in-judging-chilean-abuse-cases.cfm.

27   Fortieth Statewide Investigating Grand Jury, The Unified Judicial System of Pennsylvania, 2018.

28   Canadian Conference of Catholic Bishops, *Protecting Minors from Sexual Abuse: A Call to the Catholic Faithful in Canada for Healing, Reconciliation and Transformation* (Ottawa: CCCB Publications, 2018).

29   Pope Francis, Letter to the People of God (2018), https://www.vaticannews.va/en/pope/news/2018-08/pope-francis-letter-people-of-god-sexual-abuse.html.

30   Synod of Bishops, XV Ordinary General Assembly, *Young People, the Faith and Vocational Discernment*, Final Document, 27 October 2018, Vatican City, http://www.vatican.va/roman_curia/synod/documents/rc_synod_doc_20181027_doc-final-instrumentum-xvassemblea-giovani_en.html.

31   Pope Francis, Letter to the People of God (2018).

32   "Introduction of His Holiness Pope Francis," Meeting: The Protection of Minors in the Church," Rome, February 21, 2019, http://w2.vatican.va/content/francesco/en/speeches/2019/february/documents/papa-francesco_20190221_incontro-protezioneminori-apertura.html#INTRODUCTION_OF_HIS_HOLINESS_POPE_FRANCIS.

33   Benedict XVI, "The Church and the Scandal of Sexual Abuse," Catholic News Agency, April 10, 2019, https://www.catholicnewsagency.com/news/full-text-of-benedict-xvi-the-church-and-the-scandal-of-sexual-abuse-59639.

34   Congregation for Bishops, *Directory for the Pastoral Ministry of Bishops Apostolorum Successores* (2004), no. 226, http://www.vatican.va/roman_curia/congregations/cbishops/documents/rc_con_cbishops_doc_20040222_apostolorum-successores_en.html.

35   Pope Francis, Apostolic Letter issued motu proprio, "Vos Estis Lux Mundi" (2019), http://w2.vatican.va/content/francesco/en/motu_proprio/documents/papa-francesco-motu-proprio-20190507_vos-estis-lux-mundi.html.

36   Joshua J. McElwee, "Francis: Decision on women deacons cannot be made 'without historical foundation,'" *National Catholic Reporter*, May 10, 2019, https://www.ncronline.org/news/vatican/francis-decision-women-deacons-cannot-be-made-without-historical-foundation.

Chapter 2

1   John E. B. Myers, *Child Protection in America: Past, Present, and Future* (New York: Oxford University Press, 2006).

2   The International Society for the Prevention of Child Abuse & Neglect (ISPCAN), *World Perspectives on Child Abuse*, 13th ed. (Aurora, CO: ISPCAN Press, 2018).

3   Mary Gail Frawley-O'Dea, *Perversion of Power: Sexual Abuse in the Catholic Church* (Nashville, TN: Vanderbilt University, 2007).

4   Gary Bergeron, *Don't Call Me a Victim* (Lowell, MA: King Printing Company, 2004); Hank Estrada, *UnHoly Communion: Lessons Learned from Life Among Pedophiles, Predators, and Priests* (New Mexico: Red Rabbit Press, 2011); Carmine Galasso, *Crosses: Portraits of Clergy Abuse* (London: Trolley Ltd., 2007); Tony Lembo, *The Hopeville Fire Department: A Boy's Tale of Betrayal by One of New England's Most Notorious Priests* (Doylestown, PA: Prose & Pictures, 2007); Colm O'Gorman, *Beyond Belief* (London: Hodder & Stoughton, 2010); David Price, *Altar Boy, Altered Life: A True Story of Sexual Abuse* (Indianapolis, IN: Dog Ear Publishing, 2008).

5   David Finkelhor and Angela Browne, "The Traumatic Impact of Child Sexual Abuse: A Conceptualization," *American Journal of Orthopsychiatry* 55:4 (October 1985): 530–41.

6   Stephen J. Rossetti, "The Impact of Child Sexual Abuse on Attitudes toward God and the Catholic Church," *Child Abuse & Neglect* 19:12 (1995): 1469–81; Thomas P. Doyle, "The Spiritual Trauma Experienced by Victims of Sexual Abuse by Catholic Clergy," *Pastoral Psychology* 58 (2009): 239–60.

7   Leslie H. Wind, James M. Sullivan and Daniel J. Levins, "Survivors' Perspectives on the Impact of Clergy Sexual Abuse on Families of Origin," *Journal of Child Sexual Abuse* 17:3–4 (2008): 238–54.

8   Paul M. Kline, Robert McMackin and Edna Lezotte, "The Impact of the Clergy Abuse Scandal on Parish Communities," *Journal of Child Sexual Abuse* 17:3–4 (2008): 290–300.

9   Philip Jenkins, *Moral Panic: Changing Concepts of the Child Molester in Modern America* (New Haven, CT: Yale University Press, 2004).

10   David Finkelhor, *Child Sexual Abuse: New Theory and Research* (New York: Free Press, 1984).

11   Eugene C. Kennedy and Victor J. Heckler, *The Catholic Priest in the United States: Psychological Investigations* (Washington, DC: United States Catholic Conference Publications Office, 1972).

12   Gerard J. McGlone and Len Sperry, *The Inner Life of Priests* (Collegeville, MN: Liturgical Press, 2012).

13   Pope John Paul II, Post-Synodal Exhortation *Pastores Dabo Vobis*, To the Bishops, Clergy and Faithful on the Formation of Priests in the Circumstances of the Present Day, 1992, http://w2.vatican.va/content/john-paul-ii/en/apost_exhortations/documents/hf_jp-ii_exh_25031992_pastores-dabo-vobis.html.

14   John Jay College of Criminal Justice, Catholic Church and United States Conference of Catholic Bishops, *The Nature and Scope of Sexual Abuse of Minors by Catholic Priests and Deacons in the United States, 1950–2002* (Washington, DC: United States Conference of Catholic Bishops, 2004).

15   Mary Gail Frawley-O'Dea, *Perversion of Power: Sexual Abuse in the Catholic Church*, 1st ed. (Nashville, TN: Vanderbilt University, 2007).

16   Paul A. Holmes, "Sacramental Psychology: Treating Intimacy Failure in Catholic Priests," *Journal of Religion and Health* 35 (1996): 125–40.

17   Leon J. Podles, *Sacrilege: Sexual Abuse in the Catholic Church* (Baltimore, MD: Crossland Press, 2008).

18   Peter Steinfels, *A People Adrift: The Crisis of the Roman Catholic Church in America* (New York: Simon & Schuster, 2008), 46.

19   James F. Keenan, *A History of Catholic Moral Theology in the Twentieth Century: From Confessing Sins to Liberating Conscience* (New York: Continuum, 2010).

20   Richard A. McCormick, "Moral Theology 1940–1989: An Overview," in *The Historical Development of Fundamental Moral Theology in the United States*, eds. Charles E. Curran and Richard A. McCormick (New York: Paulist Press, 1999), 46–74.

21   John Mahoney, *The Making of Moral Theology: A Study of the Roman Catholic Tradition* (Oxford: Clarendon Press, 2006).

22   Bernhard Häring, *The Law of Christ: Moral Theology for Priests and Laity, Vols. I–III*, trans. Edwin G. Kaiser (Westminster, MD: Newman Press, 1967), vii.

23   *Dignitatis Humanae*, On the Right of the Person and of Communities to Social and Civil Freedom in Matters Religious (1965), no. 3, http://www.vatican.va/archive/ hist_councils/ii_vatican_council/documents/vat-ii_decl_19651207_dignitatis- humanae_en.html.

24   Daniel Harrington and James Keenan, *Jesus and Virtue Ethics: Building Bridges between New Testament Studies and Moral Theology* (Lanham, MD: Sheed & Ward, 2002).

25   Harrington and Keenan, *Jesus and Virtue Ethics*, 73.

26   Pope Leo XIII, Encyclical *Rerum Novarum*, On Capital and Labor (1891), http:// w2.vatican.va/content/leo-xiii/en/encyclicals/documents/hf_l-xiii_enc_15051891_ rerum-novarum.html.

27   Norbert J. Rigali, "Moral Theology and Church Responses to Sexual Abuse," *Horizons* 34 (2007): 183–204.

28   Anne E. Patrick, *Liberating Conscience: Feminist Explorations in Catholic Moral Theology* (New York: Continuum, 1996).

29   Carol Gilligan, *In a Different Voice: Psychological Theory and Women's Development* (Cambridge, MA: Harvard University Press, 1982).

30   Sandra M. Schneiders, *Beyond Patching: Faith and Feminism in the Catholic Church* (Mahwah, NJ: Paulist Press, 1991).

31   Anne M. Clifford, *Introducing Feminist Theology* (Maryknoll, NY: Orbis Books, 2001).

32   Lisa Sowle Cahill, "Feminist Theology and a Participatory Church," in *Common Calling: The Laity and Governance of the Catholic Church*, ed. Stephen J. Pope (Washington, DC: Georgetown University Press, 2004), 117–50.

33   Margaret A. Farley, *Just Love: A Framework for Christian Sexual Ethics* (New York: Continuum, 2012).

34   Karl Rahner, "Ideas for a Theology of Childhood," in *Theological Investigations*, vol. 8: *Further Theology of the Spiritual Life 2* (London: Darton, Longman & Todd, 1971), 33–50.

35   Marcia J. Bunge, ed., *The Child in the Bible* (Grand Rapids, MI: Eerdmans, 2008).

Chapter 3

1   Michael D. White and Karen J. Terry, "Child Sexual Abuse in the Catholic Church: Revisiting the Rotten Apples Explanation," *Criminal Justice and Behavior* 35:5 (2008): 658–78 at 667.

2   Gerard J. McGlone and Len Sperry, *The Inner Life of Priests* (Collegeville, MN: Liturgical Press, 2012), 41.

3   Jean M. Bartunek, Mary Ann Hinsdale and James F. Keenan, *Church Ethics and Its Organizational Context: Learning from the Sex Abuse Scandal in the Catholic Church* (Lanham, MD: Rowman and Littlefield, 2006).

4   Marie Keenan, *Child Sexual Abuse and the Catholic Church: Gender, Power, and Organizational Culture* (New York: Oxford University Press, 2012), xxvi.

5   Regina Ammicht-Quinn, Hille Haker and Maureen Junker-Kenny, *The Structural Betrayal of Trust*, 3rd ed. (London: SCM Press, 2004).

6   Thomas P. Doyle, "Clericalism: Enabler of Clergy Sexual Abuse," *Pastoral Psychology* 54 (2006): 189–213 at 201.

7   Brian P. Flanagan, *Stumbling in Holiness: Sin and Sanctity in the Church* (Collegeville, MN: Liturgical Press Academic, 2018).

8   George Weigel, *The Courage to Be Catholic: Crisis, Reform and the Future of the Church* (New York: Basic Books, 2002).

9   Lisa Sowle Cahill, "Feminist Theology and a Participatory Church," in *Common Calling: The Laity and Governance of the Catholic Church*, ed. Stephen J. Pope (Washington, DC: Georgetown University Press, 2004), 117–50.

10   Anne M. Clifford, *Introducing Feminist Theology* (Maryknoll, NY: Orbis Books, 2001).

11   Leslie M. Lothstein, "Men of the Flesh: The Evaluation and Treatment of Sexually Abusing Priests," *Studies in Gender and Sexuality* 5 (2004): 167–95 at 172.

12   Norbert J. Rigali, "Moral Theology and Church Responses to Sexual Abuse," *Horizons* 34:2 (2007): 183–204.

13   Cristina L. H. Traina, "Sex in the City of God," *Currents in Theology and Mission* 30 (2003): 5–19.

14 Lisa Sowle Cahill, John Garvey and T. Frank Kennedy, *Sexuality and the U.S. Catholic Church: Crisis and Renewal* (New York: Crossroad, 2006); James F. Keenan, "Notes on Moral Theology: Ethics and the Crisis in the Church," *Theological Studies* 66 (2005):117–36.

15 Todd A. Salzman and Michael G. Lawler, *The Sexual Person: Toward a Renewed Catholic Anthropology* (Washington, DC: Georgetown University Press, 2008).

16 Todd A. Salzman and Michael G. Lawler, "*Amoris Laetitia*: Towards a Methodological and Anthropological Integration of Catholic Sexual Ethics," *Theological Studies* 79:3 (2018): 634–52.

17 Pope Paul VI, Encyclical Letter *Humanae Vitae* (1968), http://w2.vatican.va/content/paul-vi/en/encyclicals/documents/hf_p-vi_enc_25071968_humanae-vitae.html.

18 Norbert J. Rigali, "On the *Humanae Vitae* Process: Ethics of Teaching Morality," *Louvain Studies* 2 (1998): 3–21.

19 Pope John Paul II, *The Theology of the Body: Human Love in the Divine Plan* (Boston: Pauline Books & Media, 1997).

20 Richard R. Gaillardetz, *Ecclesiology for a Global Church: A People Called and Sent* (Maryknoll, NY: Orbis, 2008), 35.

21 Cardinal Joseph Bernardin and Archbishop Oscar H. Lipscomb, *Catholic Common Ground Initiative: Foundational Documents* (New York: Crossroad, 1997), 40.

Chapter 4

1 Jay Katz, *The Silent World of Doctor and Patient* (New York: The Free Press, 1984).

2 Donald Cozzens, *Sacred Silence: Denial and Crisis in the Church* (Collegeville, MN: Liturgical Press, 2002), 25.

3 Eviatar Zerubavel, *The Elephant in the Room: Silence and Denial in Ordinary Life* (New York: Oxford University Press, 2006), 4.

4 Angela Senander, *Scandal: The Catholic Church and Public Life* (Collegeville, MN: Liturgical Press, 2012).

5 Timothy D. Lytton, *Holding Bishops Accountable: How Lawsuits Helped the Catholic Church Confront Clergy Sexual Abuse* (Cambridge, MA: Harvard University, 2008).

6 Sissela Bok, *Secrets: On the Ethics of Concealment and Revelation* (New York: Vintage Books, 1983).

7 Dan Bar-On, *The Indescribable and the Undiscussable: Reconstructing Human Discourse after Trauma* (Baltimore, MD: Central European University Press, 1999).

8 Zerubavel, *The Elephant in the Room.*

9 C. Fred Alford, *Whistleblowers: Broken Lives and Organizational Power* (New York: Cornell University Press, 2001).

10 Marcia P. Miceli, Janet P. Near and Terry Morehead Dworkin, eds., *Whistleblowing in Organizations* (New York: Routledge, 2008).

11   Paul Tracey, Nelson Phillips and Michael Lounsbury, eds., *Religion and Organization Theory: Research in the Sociology of Organizations*, vol. 41 (Bingley, UK: Emerald Publishing, 2014).

12   Kent D. Miller, "Organizational Research as Practical Theology," *Organizational Research Methods* 18 (2015): 276–99.

13   Tom Barth, "Crisis Management in the Catholic Church: Lessons for Public Administrators," *Public Administration Review* 70 (2010): 780–91.

14   Brad S. Long and Cathy Driscoll, "Codes of Ethics and the Pursuit of Organizational Legitimacy: Theoretical and Empirical Contributions," *Journal of Business Ethics* 77 (2007): 173–89, at 173.

15   Diane Vaughan, "The Dark Side of Organizations: Mistake, Misconduct, and Disaster," *Annual Review of Sociology* 25 (1999): 271–305.

16   Elizabeth Wolfe Morrison and Frances J. Milliken, "Organizational Silence: A Barrier to Change and Development in a Pluralistic World," *Academy of Management Review* 25 (2000): 706–25 at 708.

17   Edgar H. Schein, *Organizational Culture and Leadership* (San Francisco: Jossey-Bass, 1985).

18   Kelly E. See, Elizabeth W. Morrison, Naomi B. Rothman and Jack B. Soll, "The Detrimental Effects of Power on Confidence, Advice Taking and Accuracy," *Organizational Behavior and Human Decision Processes* 116 (2011): 272–85.

19   Cozzens, *Sacred Silence*.

20   Jean M. Bartunek, "The Sexual Abuse Scandal as Social Drama," in *Church Ethics and Its Organizational Context: Learning from the Sex Abuse Scandal in the Catholic Church*, eds. Jean M. Bartunek, Mary Ann Hinsdale and James F. Keenan (Lanham, MD: Rowman & Littlefield, 2006), 17–28.

21   Frederick Bruce Bird, *The Muted Conscience: Moral Silence and the Practice of Ethics in Business* (New York: Praeger, 2002).

22   Malikeh Beheshtifar, Hossein Borhani and Mahmood Moghadam, "Destructive Role of Employee Silence in Organizational Success," *International Journal of Academic Research in Business and Social Sciences* 2 (2012): 275–82.

23   John Mahoney, *The Making of Moral Theology: A Study of the Roman Catholic Tradition* (New York: Oxford University Press, 1987); James F. Keenan, *A History of Catholic Moral Theology in the Twentieth Century: From Confessing Sins to Liberating Consciences* (London: Continuum, 2010).

24   Kieran Tapsell, *Potiphar's Wife: The Vatican's Secret and Child Sexual Abuse* (Adelaide, Australia: ATF Press, 2014).

25   Brian P. Flanagan, *Stumbling in Holiness: Sin and Sanctity in the Church* (Collegeville, MN: Liturgical Press Academic, 2018).

26   Richard M. Gula, "A Professional Code of Ethics?" in *Church Ethics and Its Organizational Context: Learning from the Sex Abuse Scandal in the Catholic Church*, eds. Jean M. Bartunek, Mary Ann Hinsdale and James F. Keenan (Lanham, MD: Rowman & Littlefield, 2006), 147–56.

27   Charles E. Curran, *Loyal Dissent: Memoir of a Catholic Theologian* (Washington, DC: Georgetown University Press, 2006).

28   Conference of Major Superiors of Men, 2007, in Mary Gail Frawley-O'Dea, *Perversion of Power: Sexual Abuse in the Catholic Church* (Nashville, TN: Vanderbilt University, 2007), 151.

29   Thomas P. Doyle, A.W. Richard Sipe and Patrick J. Wall, *Sex, Priests, and Secret Codes: The Catholic Church's 2000-Year Paper Trail of Sexual Abuse* (Los Angeles: Volt Press, 2006), 21.

30   Gary Wills, *Papal Sin: Structures of Deceit* (New York: Image Books, 2000).

31   R. R. Gaillardetz, *When the Magisterium Intervenes: The Magisterium and Theologians in Today's Church* (Collegeville, MN: Liturgical Press, 2012).

32   Robert Blair Kaiser, *Whistle: Fr. Tom Doyle's Steadfast Witness for Victims of Clerical Sexual Abuse* (CreateSpace Independent Publishing Platform, 2015).

33   Bradford Hinze, *Practices of Dialogue in the Roman Catholic Church: Aims, Obstacles, Lessons and Laments* (New York: Continuum, 2006).

34   Dogmatic Constitution on the Church, *Lumen Gentium* (1964), no. 37, http://www.vatican.va/archive/hist_councils/ii_vatican_council/documents/vat-ii_const_19641121_lumen-gentium_en.html.

35   Cardinal Joseph Bernardin and Archbishop Oscar H. Lipscomb, *Catholic Common Ground Initiative: Foundational Documents* (New York: Crossroad, 1997), 42–44.

36   Bradford E. Hinze, "Ecclesial Repentance and the Demands of Dialogue," *Theological Studies* 61 (2000): 207–38 at 213.

Chapter 5

1   Peter Damiean, *The Book of Gomorrah and St. Peter Damian's Struggle Against Ecclesiastical Corruption*, trans. Matthew Cullinan Hoffman (Ite ad Thomam Books and Media, 2015).

2   Thomas E. Woods Jr., *The Church Confronts Modernity: Catholic Intellectuals and the Progressive Era* (New York: Columbia University Press, 2006).

3   Pope Leo XIII, *Immortale Dei,* On the Christian Constitution of States (1885), nos. 8 and 35, http://w2.vatican.va/content/leo-xiii/en/encyclicals/documents/hf_l-xiii_enc_01111885_immortale-dei.html.

4   William T. Cavanaugh, *Migrations of the Holy: Theologies of Church and State* (Grand Rapids, MI: Eerdmans, 2011).

5   John W. O'Malley, *What Happened at Vatican II* (Cambridge, MA: The Belknap Press, 2008).

Chapter 6

1   Acton Institute, https://acton.org/research/lord-acton-quote-archive.

2   Timothy D. Lytton, *Holding Bishops Accountable: How Lawsuits Helped the Catholic Church Confront Clergy Sexual Abuse* (Cambridge, MA: Harvard University Press, 2008); Joseph P. Chinnici, *When Values Collide: The Catholic Church, Sexual Abuse, and the Challenges of Leadership* (Maryknoll, NY: Orbis Books, 2010).

3   Stephen Bullivant, Eric Marcelo O. Genilo, Daniel Franklin Pilario and Agnes M. Brazal, eds., *Theology and Power: International Perspectives* (Mahwah, NJ: Paulist Press, 2016).

4   Mary Gail Frawley-O'Dea, *Perversion of Power: Sexual Abuse in the Catholic Church* (Nashville, TN: Vanderbilt University, 2007).

5   Jason Berry and Gerald Renner, *Vows of Silence: The Abuse of Power in the Papacy of John Paul II* (New York: Free Press, 2004).

6   Michael W. Higgins and Douglas R. Letson, *Power and Peril: The Catholic Church at the Crossroads* (Toronto: Harper Collins, 2002).

7   Geoffrey Robinson, *Confronting Power and Sex in the Catholic Church* (Collegeville, MN: Liturgical Press, 2008).

8   Irish Catholic Bishops Conference, "Statement from the Winter General Meeting of the Irish Bishops' Conference" (2009), https://www.catholicbishops.ie/2009/12/09/statement-winter-general-meeting-irish-bishops-conference.

9   Michael L. Papesh, *Clerical Culture: Contradiction and Transformation: The Culture of the Diocesan Priests of the United States Catholic Church* (Collegeville, MN: Liturgical Press, 2004).

10 Michael Paul Gallagher, *Clashing Cymbals: An Introduction to Faith and Culture* (New York: Paulist Press, 2003).

11 Edgar H. Schein, *Organizational Culture and Leadership* (San Francisco: Jossey-Bass, 1985).

12 Kelly E. See, Elizabeth W. Morrison, Naomi B. Rothman and Jack B. Soll, "The Detrimental Effects of Power on Confidence, Advice Taking and Accuracy," *Organizational Behavior and Human Decision Processes* 116 (2011): 272–85.

13 Chris Argyris, *Overcoming Organizational Defenses: Facilitating Organizational Learning* (Needham Heights, MA: Allyn and Bacon, 1990).

14 Gerald A. Arbuckle, *Dealing with Bullies: A Gospel Response to the Social Disease of Adult Bullying* (Strathfield, NSW: St Paul's Publications, 2003).

15 Papesh, *Clerical Culture*, 21.

16 Thomas F. O'Meara, *Theology of Ministry*, 2nd ed. (New York: Paulist Press, 1999), 102.

17 Papesh, *Clerical Culture*, 36.

18 O'Meara, *Theology of Ministry*; Paul Bernier, *Ministry in the Church: A Historical and Pastoral Approach* (Mystic, CT: Twenty-Third Publications, 1992).

19   Paul Lakeland, *The Liberation of the Laity: In Search of an Accountable Church* (New York: Continuum, 2004).

20   Pope Francis, Letter to the People of God (2018), https://www.vaticannews.va/en/pope/news/2018-08/pope-francis-letter-people-of-god-sexual-abuse.html.

21   Conference of Major Superiors of Men, *In Solidarity and Service: Reflections on the Problem of Clericalism in the Church* (Washington, DC, 1983), 2.

22   George B. Wilson, *Clericalism: The Death of the Priesthood* (Collegeville, MN: Liturgical Press, 2008).

23   Donald B. Cozzens, *Sacred Silence: Denial and the Crisis in the Church* (Collegeville, MN: Liturgical Press, 2002).

24   Thomas P. Doyle, "Clericalism and Catholic Clergy Sexual Abuse," in *Predatory Priests, Silenced Victims: The Sexual Abuse Crisis and the Catholic Church*, eds. Mary Gail Frawley-O'Dea and Virginia Goldner (Mahwah, NJ: The Analytic Press, 2007), 147–62 at 158.

25   Peter Steinfels, *A People Adrift: The Crisis of the Roman Catholic Church in America* (New York: Simon & Schuster, 2008), 46.

26   "To Serve the People of God: Renewing the Conversation on Priesthood and Ministry," Boston College Seminar on Priesthood and Ministry for the Contemporary Church, *Origins 48:31* (December 27, 2018): 484–93.

27   "Final Document of the Synod of Bishops on Young People, Faith and Vocational Discernment," 2018, no. 148, http://www.synod2018.va/content/synod2018/en/fede-discernimento-vocazione/final-document-of-the-synod-of-bishops-on-young-people--faith-an.html.

28   Christine Schenk, *Crispina and Her Sisters: Women and Authority in Early Christianity* (Minneapolis, MN: Fortress Press, 2017).

29   Sandra M. Schneiders, *Beyond Patching: Faith and Feminism in the Catholic Church* (Mahwah, NJ: Paulist Press, 1991).

Chapter 7

1   Brad Gregory, *The Unintended Reformation: How a Religious Revolution Secularized Society* (Cambridge, MA: The Belknap Press, 2015).

2   Richard Gaillardetz and Catherine Clifford, *Keys to the Council: Unlocking the Teaching of Vatican II* (Collegeville, MN: Liturgical Press, 2012).

3   Immanuel Kant, *Prolegomena to Any Future Metaphysics that Will Be Able to Come Forward as Science*, trans. Gary Hatfield (Cambridge, MA: Cambridge University Press, 2004): 4, 260, 10.

4   Immanuel Kant, *Perpetual Peace: A Philosophical Essay, 1795,* https://www.gutenberg.org/ebooks/50922.

5   Thomas P. Rausch, *Towards a Truly Catholic Church: An Ecclesiology for the Third Millennium* (Collegeville, MN: Liturgical Press, 2005).

Chapter 8

1   International Theological Commission, "Memory and Reconciliation: The Church and the Faults of the Past," *Origins* 29:39 (March 16, 2000): 625–44 at 628.

2   Keith Michael Hearit, *Crisis Management by Apology: Corporate Responses to Wrongdoing* (Mahwah, NJ: Lawrence Erlbaum, 2006).

3   Bradford E. Hinze, "Ecclesial Repentance and the Demands of Dialogue," *Theological Studies* 61 (2000): 207–38 at 208.

4   Joseph Ratzinger, *Called to Communion: Understanding the Church Today*, trans. Adrian Walker (San Francisco: Ignatius Press, 1996), 162.

5   Richard R. Gaillardetz, *Ecclesiology for a Global Church: A People Called and Sent* (Maryknoll, NY: Orbis Books, 2008).

6   Pope John Paul II, *Ecclesia in Oceania*, Libreria Editrice Vaticana (November 22, 2001).

7   Benedict XVI, Address of His Holiness Benedict XVI on the Occasion of Christmas Greetings to the Roman Curia, Libreria Editrice Vaticana, December 20, 2010.

8   Pope Francis, Post-Synodal Apostolic Exhortation *Amoris Laetitia, On Love in the Family* (2016), no. 300, https://w2.vatican.va/content/dam/francesco/pdf/apost_exhortations/documents/papa-francesco_esortazione-ap_20160319_amoris-laetitia_en.pdf.

9   Katarina Schuth, *Seminary Formation: Recent History, Current Circumstances, New Directions* (Collegeville, MN: Liturgical Press, 2016).

10 Boston College Seminar, "To Serve the People of God: Renewing the Conversation on Priesthood and Ministry," *Origins* 48:31 (December 27, 2018): 484–93.

11 Catholic Partnership Summit, *Heal the Body of Christ: A Plan to Create a New Culture of Leadership and New Response to Abuse in the Catholic Church* (Washington, DC: Leadership Roundtable, 2019), https://leadershiproundtable.org/wp-content/uploads.

12 Massimo Faggioli, "Hierarchy and Theology Alike Are Caught up in Catholic Disruption," June 7, 2019, https://www.ncronline.org/news/accountability/hierarchy-and-theology-alike-are-caught-catholic-disruption.

13 Pontifical Gregorian University Centre for Child Protection, "Doing Theology in the Face of Sexual Abuse." Personal correspondence.

14 John L. Allen Jr., *The Future Church: How Ten Trends Are Revolutionizing the Catholic Church* (New York: Image Books, 2009).

15 Donald Cozzens, *Sacred Silence: Denial and Crisis in the Church* (Collegeville, MN: Liturgical Press, 2002) 25.

MARQUIS

Québec, Canada